I0137497

EAT YOUR Ps

EAT YOUR Ps

William Carter, Jr.

CrossLink Publishing

Copyright © 2018 William Carter, Jr.

All rights reserved. No part of this publication may be reproduced, distributed or transmitted in any form or by any means, including photocopying, recording, or other electronic or mechanical methods, without the prior written permission of the publisher, except in the case of brief quotations embodied in critical reviews and certain other non-commercial uses permitted by copyright law. For permission requests, write to the publisher, addressed "Attention: Permissions Coordinator," at the address below.

CrossLink Publishing
558 E. Castle Pines Pkwy, Ste B4117
Castle Rock, CO 80108
www.crosslinkpublishing.com

Ordering Information:
Quantity sales. Special discounts are available on quantity purchases by corporations, associations, and others. For details, contact the "Special Sales Department" at the address above.

Eat Your Ps/Carter —1st ed.

ISBN 978-1-63357-151-8

Library of Congress Control Number: 2018946974

First edition: 10 9 8 7 6 5 4 3 2 1

All scripture quotations are taken from the Holy Bible, King James Version (Public Domain).

'If Peas Could Taste Like Candy" taken from **If Peas Could Taste Like Candy** by **Crystal Bowman**, Copyright © **1998** by **Crystal Bowman**. Used by permission of Zonderava. www.zondervan.com.

"I am very impressed! There's a lesson to be learned for all who read this book and the lifestyle depicted is a plus for everyone."

- Deacon Vernon Winfrey (Oprah's Dad)
Faith United Baptist Church
Nashville, TN

"I've never been so pleased with peas until I read about Pastor Carter's p's! This is a very thought-provoking, profound, inspiring, exhilarating, and well-written book."

-Reverend Dr. E. Theophilus Caviness
President of the Southern Christian Leadership Conference
Cleveland, OH

"Pastor Carter proves to be an excellent teacher who captivates his audience. This book serves as the perfect 'how-to' guide for a well-balanced spiritual diet. Eat Your Ps will leave you with an internal PEAce that surpasses all understanding."

-Karen P. Knowles, MD
Internal Medicine Specialist
Nashville, TN

"Eat Your Ps is an outstanding work written by an outstanding young man! Although I love peas, the p's written about in this book will help any human being excel spiritually. Every Christian must eat Praise, Purging, Prayers, Promises, Persecution, Proverbs, and Purpose. Without making these concepts applicable to your daily lives, you will never reach the zenith of your spiritual success. I strongly encourage each of you to read this book and allow it to minister to your soul, for it is supported 100% by the Word of God. I was truly inspired, motivated, and encouraged and pray that you will be also."

-Bishop Gilbert L. Evans, Jr., J.D., Ph. D
Vice President & Assistant General
Counsel at St. Johns River State College
Senior Pastor of The House of God Church
Palatka, FL

"Comparing the Christian life to eating a variety of peas may seem a bit unorthodox until you dig into the pages and see the purpose and wisdom of the analogy. Whether you are Baptist, Pentecostal, Presbyterian, or another denomination, the biblical principles creatively outlined in this book will deepen your spiritual journey and bring closer to your heavenly Father."

-Crystal Bowman
Best-selling, award winning author of more than 100 books
including Our Daily Bread for Kids, Does God Take Naps?
and M is for Manger

"William Carter, Jr. has masterfully combined his commendable communication skills with homiletic resonance in his book Eat

Your P's! Each chapter reads with the likeness of a multi-piece classical music arrangement which builds as it moves, depositing the uncommon warmth of transparency from his personal life coupled with his never disappointing yet apt command of Scripture. The conversational tone of William's penmanship is the contagion of this book, yielding down-to-earth wisdom that's theologically sound and practically attainable. Enjoy this profoundly engaging, intelligently arranged, and marvelously adept mine of wisdom. It is informative, disciple-worthy, and an excellent tool for trans-generational and trans-denominational audiences."

-Wayne R. Felton
The Archbishop of, Communion of Holy Christian Churches
The Senior Pastor of, The Holy Christian Cathedral
Saint Paul, MN

"Bold, original, authentic. Pastor Carter genuinely cares for the hearts of people. I pray this book begins a greater dialogue on cross-cultural discipleship within the broader Evangelical community."

—Dr. Clary Butler, Jr.
Professor of Graduate Studies in Christian Leadership and
Organizational Development
Trinity International University
Pastor and Director for Young Professionals, Young Couples
and College Students
Willow Creek Community Church, Greater Chicago, IL

"This is one of the warmest, most genuine, and personal books I have read in a long time. William's heart-felt love for God and family come through on every page. If you are looking for an unswervingly Biblical book that will both encourage and challenge, you will find it in these pages. The lessons can be immediately applied and William is such a deeply joyful person that it's hard not to feel like you're walking with a friend when you read his words. I highly recommend this book!"

-Chris Reid
Discipleship and Connection Minister
The Church at Woodbine; Regional Campus of Brentwood
Baptist Church, Brentwood, TN

DEDICATION

This book is dedicated to my father, William B. Carter, Sr. Far too few children get to grow up having both parents in the household like I did. Even fewer are reared in the fear and admonition of the Lord. When you toss in the negative statistics regarding African American boys, the fact that I didn't wind up incarcerated, in a gang or without a high school diploma puts me in an even smaller category.

I didn't realize how much Pops had poured into me until I started writing, and the words just kept flowing. He was and still is a spiritual example of integrity and consistency. I am grateful that he pushed me to do my best. I now appreciate how he disciplined me and was determined to keep me from becoming just another statistic. Although, a flawed vessel, I am eternally grateful for everything I am, everything I'm not, and everything I hope to be. My father equipped me with both the tools and the tenacity I would need to succeed.

He chose a wife who was an awesome mother to each of his children. We miss her dearly but would be selfishly incorrect to say she left before her work was done. She reared us well. She poured immeasurable greatness into her children and many others whom she came to know.

I'm so glad my Pops readily approved of the girl I brought home and later made my wife. He was hard on us with regard to such. I'll never forget his deep concern when he met one of my friends whom he deemed less-desirable. He was relieved to learn that we were merely friends, and I was not dating her. Thank God I stumbled upon quite a jewel and immediately got his personal endorsement.

It would be impossible to try to repay him for all that he is to our family. But, I hope in some small way that this publication makes him half as proud as I am to honor him as my father.

EPIGRAPH

...read its contents prayerfully and carefully in the name of the Lord, and we believe you shall, if of honest hearts, acknowledge them to be of much benefit and value to all...

Saint Mother Mary Magdalena Lewis Tate

The righteous eateth to the satisfying of his soul

Proverbs 13:25a

If Peas Could Taste Like Candy

Dear God, please bless this dinner
That we're about to eat.
And with your special blessing,
Please make the food taste sweet.

If peas could taste like candy,
And fish like chocolate pie,
Then I'd gladly eat my dinner.
So please, God, could you try?

If my milk could taste like Kook-Aid,
Dear God, I know you're able,
It'd make me very thankful
For the food that's on the table.

If you could add some sugar,
I don't think that would hurt.
'Cause if I eat my dinner,
I get to have dessert.

Contents

FOREWORD

*E*at Your P's tells us a lot about spirituality. Cultivating and extracting from the soil of his experiences, William Carter opens a treasure trove of spiritual insight for the holistic sustaining of spiritual health for mind, body, and soul. Raised in an agricultural tradition of farming and gardening, the author of Eat Your P's has crafted perceptible parables with profound insight to grasp the relational quality of God's love and life in our human quest for authentic existence. In the simple stories found in this exegetical memoir, the reader finds clear metaphorical symbolism for a daily diet to embody a relevant spirituality that keeps life close to the purposes of God. As the metabolic ingredients in peas work wonders for the health of the body, a daily menu of holistic spirituality and praise of God will keep one's life stitched to God, love of self and love of neighbor.

This book is an immensely important devotional guide for deepening faith and spirituality against a culture of individualism and diminishing appreciation for the communal qualities of life. Discovering the life of God in oneself is inextricably linked to discovering God in the life of others. The beauty of creation and in the diverse display of divine and human love all around us, eating the P's of spirituality has liberating and spiritual power to transform lives.

Without the menu of the P's' spirituality, as intimately crafted in this book, one can expect a famine of the soul, which will inevitably affect the spiritual health of a whole nation. The disciplines of the spirit that keeps the heart warm for loving justice, offering hospitality to strangers, and being an agent for God's work in the world will suffer or go completely lacking without this solid diet. Eat Your P's is a gift for the table of our humanity and collective soul.

Dr. Forrest E. Harris, Sr.
American Baptist College, President
Vanderbilt Divinity School, Associate Professor of the Practice of Ministry
Chicago Theological Seminary, Board of Trustees
Published author of 3 Non-fiction religious books

ACKNOWLEDGEMENTS

God tremendously blessed me by planting seven p's within my family. Each of these women has played an intimate role in furthering me as a person, so I pause to thank God for surrounding me with their plenipotentiary power.

Nova Walker-Carter: My wife, my partner, my lover, my prized possession, my help meet, my personal editor, & my queen.

Aijalon Carter: My baby, my only offspring, my pride, my joy, my greatest accomplishment, my defender, & my Bouggie.

The Late Rebecca Carter: My mother, my nurturer, my teacher, my encourager, my source, my example, & my refuge.

The Late Theresa Carter: My big sister, my #1 fan, my first 2nd mom, my cook, my laughter, my protector, & my mouthpiece.

The Late Lorena Carter: My grandmother, my foundation, my tradition-setter, my bounty, my example of love, my songbird, & my prayer warrior.

The Late Willette "Tena" Walker: My mother-in-law, my partner in crime, my confidant, my positive reinforcement, my wellspring, my safe haven, & my peace maker.

Rosa Mae Walker: My grandmother-in-law, my giving tree, my private chef, my constant help, my home away from home, my cheerleader, & my genuine friend.

I express my heartfelt gratitude for the sacrificial time **each of my endorsers** spent to share in the furtherance of this publication. It became a greater book because of them. I thank the **House Of God Church** family as well as the **Bakers Chapel CME Church** family for helping to provide my spiritual foundation while allowing and encouraging me to use my talents and gifts for His glory. Special thanks to **Michael Randolph** and **Marcia McCoy** for connecting me with great people. However, being connected with the two of them is even greater. May God grant perpetual blessings and favor to **CrossLink Publishing** for seeing something in me that other agents and publishers didn't or perhaps couldn't see. **Rick Bates** and the amazing CrossLink family of editors, designers, and marketers transformed this tedious process into an informative and exciting learning experience for me. I am fortunate and eternally grateful. Thank you to my entire family, **The Carters**, **The Mingos**, the in-laws, the adopted, the surrogates, the close friends, and each of you, too numerous to mention, for your support, prayers, love and encouragement down through the years.

INTRODUCTION

As you delve into the seven main chapters of Eat Your Ps it's going to feel as if you're reading seven different books. Each is packed with a plethora of information. In order for you to get the most out of this spiritual gardening experience, follow these cultivating rules:

1. **GRAB A HIGHLIGHTER.** Highlight the statements that inspire you. If you highlight as you go, juicy tidbits will be a lot easier to locate when you need to refer to them.

2. **DON'T SKIP THE SCRIPTURES.** Read all of the references documented throughout the book, especially the familiar ones. Each was selected and iterated for good reason. The Word of God is powerful and will condition your mind to ingest each concept as intended.

3. **DON'T RUSH TO FINISH.** Rebuke the temptation to speed read. Satan is hoping you'll overlook the very things you need the most. It is foundationally important that you begin by reading chapter one. But, after that, feel free to peruse the chapter topics and focus on whichever is of pertinent interest to your spiritual well-being. Take your time. Reread. Study. Meditate. Change is not always easy and rarely happens overnight. Consider this book a companion that will be by your side for years to come. There are no bonus points for finishing early.

4. **USE THIS BOOK AS YOUR WEAPON.** Do not give your copy away but keep it as ammunition for the mental battles you'll encounter as you seek spiritual elevation. You may not need it today. But, as you continue to grow in your walk with the Lord, I guarantee you'll eventually be challenged in each of these seven areas. At that point, re-read the applicable chapter or simply review the seven bullet points at the end of each. Maybe you'll only have time to scan your highlights but, as soon the Holy Spirit reminds you that you have this resource, use it.

5. **TELL OTHERS ABOUT THIS BOOK** if you think well of it. While books are a dime a dozen, and I've read my fair share, I can only think of a few that helped transform my life. Each time that happened, the book had come to me highly recommended, and I was inspired to tell someone else. Buy it as a gift for a new convert or a friend who is struggling in one of the seven areas. My wife bought a book for me and after I read it, I bought one for each of the married men on my ministerial staff. I also retained a few to give out when led to do so. As fellow soldiers, we owe it to our Christian brothers and sisters to help as often as we can. Discuss these concepts with your fellow Christian friends in small study groups or at church as your pastor permits.

6. **LISTEN TO AT LEAST ONE OF THE SUGGESTED SONGS** at the end of each chapter. Music has a way of touching the soul unlike anything else on the planet. I am a lifelong Gospel/Christian music guru, so the lists are quite diverse. I tried to include something for everyone's music palate. I hope you'll find at least one that's new to you. When you listen, hone in on the words of the song as they relate to the subject at hand. Even if the genre is not one you routinely listen to, try it. You might be pleasantly surprised.

7. **PROMISE YOU'LL TRY AT LEAST ONE NEW PEA** and I'm not speaking spiritually. I'm talking about the actual food in the photos at the beginning of each chapter. If you've already tried them all, find one that you and your family haven't enjoyed for a while and rediscover it as you take this journey. If you hate them all, try my personal recipe at the end of this book. I love to cook, and I think it's a pretty awesome recipe, if I don't say so myself. But either way, don't give up. Engaging this form of natural discipline will broaden your spiritual disciplinary abilities. If you are close-minded regarding food, you're probably just as close-minded spiritually, and that's not good. Push yourself beyond your personal boundaries, and you'll be amazed at what God will do in your life as a result.

CHAPTER ONE

How I Started Eating Peas

B ack in the early 1970s I grew up in a small town just north of Nashville called Goodlettsville, Tennessee: sixty-three hundred people strong. We thought of it as suburban, although our family members from Detroit, Miami, and Philadelphia never hesitated to inform us that we most definitely lived in "the country." Ugh. That was a label that I hated to wear. The stereotype for "the country" in middle Tennessee encompassed things such as running around town with no shoes on, being functionally illiterate, unable to hold an intelligent conversation, and (worst of all) incest. Needless to say, or perhaps most needful to say, for our family, these stereotypes couldn't have been further from the truth. My brother and my sisters were talented and intelligent kids. We were a strong, middle-class family, of which I was the baby; living in a cozy split-level home nestled on a corner lot with a landscape that was the envy of the neighborhood. Our parents kept us well dressed and out of trouble, and we had the audacity to be ashamed to be living in "the country." It's amazing how immaturity seems to serve as a proud platform for ignorance and is able to foster an impressive ability for an individual to detest that which should be cherished and appreciated.

My parents were humble people, so I never realized how blessed and thriving of a family we were — especially for living two blinks outside the civil rights movement in the south. Talk about making it against the odds! Our neighborhood was the only known African American community of its caliber in the quaint town of Goodlettsville, and I hadn't a clue as to why so many of my Caucasian classmates mean-mugged me on a daily basis. I wore my naivety like a badge and stuck my chest out because the elementary school principal knew me by name. He would stop in his stride, take a long stare and utter with a smile-free disposition, "Hello, William!" in a predictably baritone and monotone delivery. It happened like clockwork every time I saw him in the hallway. There were only two other black kids in my grade, and both of them lived in my neighborhood. So, I suppose I did stick out like a sore thumb. What should have been an honor became a thorn in the principal's flesh; having a black straight-A student at the prominent school. Unfortunately, he only knew me by name because my mother had to come out to the school and fight to have me placed in the advanced student program for which I'd intentionally been overlooked, and he never forgot it. Maybe he didn't know, but a few years prior, my mom participated in the nationally-acclaimed sit-ins while in college at Tennessee State University known then as Tennessee A&I. So, she "didn't take no stuff," if you will. Had it not been for Ms. Walker, an African American teacher who lived up the street and cared enough to call and inform my mother that I'd been discriminated against, she never would have known.

Middle class black people had no choice but to look out for each other back then. Our entire community felt like one big happy family. We were sheltered as kids but for all the right reasons. Had I then understood even a fraction of the things from which I was being sheltered such as drug abuse, alcoholism, and a host of criminal activity, I would have spent a lot more time enjoying and appreciating "the country" rather than trying to escape it.

Contrary to popular belief, having a fortunate upbringing did not mean we were kids who got everything we wanted. But, we always had plenty of food to enjoy, and that served as a nice buffer. My paternal grandparents are to be credited for some of that. They lived about an hour east of Goodlettsville in the Stonewall community. Stonewall is so small that it's no longer included in the census. The last inclusion was the 1895 census which counted a whopping fifty-three people. My guess is that I was related to most of them. My grandfather could have easily fed more than fifty-three with the livestock he bred and the gardens he annually cultivated. He would slaughter one of his hogs as well as one of his cows each year, and that would yield enough meat to fill his deep freezer as well as ours. That meat kept us well fed throughout the entire year.

My father also grew his own garden each year. Now, this was no ordinary small backyard garden. He took great pride in growing a wide variety of fruits and vegetables that would not only yield enough food for our six-member household but would also put food on tables throughout our community. My mother would can and freeze food until our freezers and shelves could hold no more. The rest of the food had to be given away or it would have spoiled. I remember riding through the neighborhood on the back of Dad's pickup truck, stopping at various homes, and delivering the fruit of our labor. One day I asked Dad why he didn't just sell it. He said he felt that we would receive a greater blessing from the Lord if we embraced the bounty as an opportunity to be a blessing to others. He was right, because we never ran low, and it seemed as if we could barely manage to give it all away. The blessings of the Lord were tremendous year after year. In all of those years, I never recall a year during which the garden didn't grow. I never knew rodents to completely rob us of our harvest; neither can I recall a year during which adverse weather conditions caused too much difficulty. God always plentifully provided food in what I privately referred to as, "My Daddy's Anointed Garden."

I'll never forget the year that Dad and I caught one of our well-known neighbors red-handed stealing from his garden. I was anticipating a harsh confrontation or that Dad would call the police. Instead, my father just stood there and quietly observed in disbelief. I stood near with my heart pounding as I knew Dad was carefully calculating his next move. When the neighbor had gathered about as much as he could carry and was about to make his exit, Dad shouted a friendly word of greeting. I don't remember if it was "good evening" or "hello," but it was something along those lines. Needless to say, our neighbor jumped as if he'd been struck by lightning. I'll never know if he urinated or pooped on himself. But, given the look on his face, I wouldn't have been surprised if he did both. My father had quite a skill of asking the obvious to invoke immediate self-reflection and inner shame mingled with guilt. So, of course he began his typical line of questioning as he slowly approached the man who didn't know if he should hide the greens or drop them. But, he knew it was too late to take off running. "Whatcha doin?" Dad asked, as if we didn't all know. The man tearfully apologized and confessed like a sinner on his deathbed. My father has always been a man of tremendous character. So, rather than seize this moment as an opportunity to further disdain an already remorseful soul, Dad chose to have compassion. He did, however, explain his disappointment in that he gives vegetables to everybody and told the young man that, had he only asked, he could have gotten all that he wanted. He cautioned him to not do that again, told him to leave and let him take his meager bounty right along with him. No matter how determined the man was to give them back, Dad insisted that he take all that he had unlawfully harvested.

At that very moment, I learned a life-lesson. It's interesting how we, as professed Christians, love to quote scriptures. Yet, in situations such as the one my dad happened upon, we too rarely apply them. God chose to encase a huge part of our existence on this planet in how we get along with one another. To sweeten the deal, God decided that he would reward those who bestow mercy with the mercy they will need from Him when the time comes (Matthew 5:7). And, should we choose to hold grudges and not forgive our fellowman, He will choose not to forgive us (Matthew 6:14-15). He further eradicated our right to revenge by claiming it as His own (Romans 12:19). You see, our flesh desires "eye for eye" and "tooth for tooth" when we execute judgment. However, God is Spirit and therefore, unlike us, He cannot ignore intangibles such as contrition, remorse, humility, regret and penitence. And sometimes, even when none of those emotions have come into play, God will yet have mercy, simply because He loves us unconditionally. If it is possible to baffle God, surely, He is baffled by a society that can unapologetically hang a man who is clearly sorry and begging for another chance, when He has given the hanger more second chances than can be numerated. Biblically, we are taught to LOVE mercy (Micah 6:8). But, too often, we feel as if society has been dealt an injustice if a guilty party goes unpunished for whatever he has done. Let us learn to praise God for every instance wherein mercy has been imparted and learn to love the fact that it has been shown. How dare we sit in church during Holy Week year after year and cheer for the story about the thief on the cross, whom we've never seen but cringe when our neighbor gets probation rather than a prison sentence.

Our super-garden, as I also called it, was planted on the south side of a 1.75-acre lot my father owned about a quarter of a mile from our home. During harvest season, going to the garden was like going to the grocery store. Daily we would gather the goods that seemed to have peaked and were waiting to be discovered. It was as if God literally gave us our daily bread. Over the years, my father successfully grew yellow corn, white corn, okra, ice potatoes, sweet potatoes, peanuts, broccoli, cauliflower, onions, cabbage, beans, bell peppers, turnip greens, collard greens, mustard greens, tomatoes, strawberries, cantaloupe, watermelon, cucumbers, radishes, carrots, lettuce, squash, and eggplant. There's probably more, but that's all I can recall right now. Wow, I almost forgot the yard. Our home was uniquely situated among three separate yards. Somehow, because of the shape of the corner lot, we had two front yards that were divided by cascading steps as well as the back yard and these yards looked more like a vineyard than anything. From there we enjoyed cherry tomatoes, chestnuts, pears, hazel nuts, grapes, plums and cherries. But, out of all the many items that filled the garden and yard each year, Dad grew more different types of peas than anything else. Peas, peas, and more peas filled our garden, and I always wondered why. Granted, we had both white corn and yellow corn. Sure, enough of our garden boasted of three different types of greens: collards (my Miami-native Mother's staple), turnips (my Tennessee-native Dad's staple), and mustards (just because). Dad even discovered the German tomato before it was all said and done. But, nothing outshined the annual abundance of multiple types of peas in all their glory. It was as if the entire center section of the gigantic rectangular garden was reserved just for them. It looked like we positioned a force field around them in an effort to guard them. Corn and okra stood tall on the right side of the peas. Peanuts and potatoes fenced in the bottom side, while melons and a colorful strawberry patch secured the top side. A lovely, lengthy row of green bean bushes offered shade from the left side. And throughout the inside of this geometric masterpiece, in any given year, one would be prone to encounter: pigeon peas, sugar snap peas, Crowder peas, green peas (a.k.a. garden peas), black-eyed peas, snow peas, and even cowpeas, I think. Dear God, why so many of these awful peas? I didn't even like them. They were hard to pluck. And if I had a dollar for every pea I shelled over the years, I could probably afford to give you this book for free. My mother was an awesome cook. But even she couldn't do much to improve the taste of these little horrors for me. Eventually, they grew on me, and I love all of them now. But when I was a youngster, like most kids, I'd much rather have had them off my plate than on it. My mother knew how we felt, but we dare not waste food. She also knew that peas were good for us. So, she would make dessert with every meal, and if we wanted some dessert, we each had to eat everything on our plate, including those putrid peas. Once we presented her with a clean plate, we were allowed to get dessert. Well, that was incentive enough for me to choke down the veggies unlike my sister Belinda who would find inconspicuous places in which to hide her food when Mom wasn't looking. Although I envied the fact that she had found a way to avoid eating them, I loved my sister too much to tattle.

While I was wearied by these peas that seemed pleased to present themselves regularly, little did I know how badly my body needed them. In double-checking with my father, I found that some of the peas we ate at the house, he didn't personally grow, and yet he told me of some I'd forgotten. You see, my grandfather, Woodrow Carter was an amazing gardener as well. Apparently, some of these seemingly infallible peas came from his garden. And even still, I've learned that some peas are known by multiple names. But, however they were acquired, you could bet your bottom dollar that the Carter household seldom, if ever, went pea-less.

Randy Fritz and Diana Herrington cited the pea as a powerhouse of nutrition and as a boon for our health as well as the health of the planet. Peas are low in fat but high in everything else including vital micronutrients that are rarely celebrated but quite beneficial. Peas have been cited for their preventative nature with regard to cancer, wrinkles, arthritis, osteoporosis, Alzheimer's, heart disease, and even constipation. Also, peas promote good health in multiple unique ways. As they grow, they work with the bacteria in the soil to capture nitrogen from the air and deposit it into that same soil, reducing the need for artificial fertilizers. Furthermore, what other common food do you know of that has such a diverse list of vitamins and nutrients? Vitamin B1, Vitamin B2, Vitamin B3, Vitamin B6, Vitamin K, Vitamin C, Vitamin E, high levels of antioxidants, Omega-3 fats, Omega-6 fatty acid, Iron, Magnesium, Calcium, Potassium, Folic Acid, Riboflavin, Thiamin, and Zinc are each found in peas. They even promote blood sugar regulation by reversing insulin resistance in Type 2 Diabetes. Have you ever been told that you should avoid eating green peas because of their sugar content? Well, guess what. The sugar/carbohydrate content that has caused peas to be avoided turns out to be a moot factor. The carbs in peas are natural sugars, similar to that of fruit, with no white sugars or chemicals to worry about. There are additional benefits to eating peas such as receiving the anti-inflammatory phytonutrients found almost exclusively therein which serve to prevent bone, joint and skin disorders. Wow! Who knew?

I hope that reading the benefits in the previous paragraph has motivated you to eat more peas. If we can discipline ourselves to eat what's needed for our natural bodies, we should become equally disciplined to indulge in the p's that are needed for our overall spiritual health. This book will explore seven p's that no spiritual garden should be without: *Praises, Purging, Prayer, Promises, Persecution, Proverbs, & Purpose.* Each p plays a vital role in your overall development as a Christian. Perhaps you're a brand-new convert. If so, congratulations! You'll be glad you have this book. Maybe you've been serving the Lord for more decades than you care to reveal but feel as though you've reached a spiritual plateau. You might have felt your life as a Christian was flowing well, but you've been confused as to why your life seems to be making such drastic changes and taking sharp turns. Regardless of where you are spiritually, having a solid understanding of how these p's are used by God to stablish, strengthen, and settle you (1 Peter 5:10) will catapult you so far ahead of the enemy, you'll have ample time to prepare and circumvent his snares.

Seven is regarded biblically as a number that signifies completion. Once you comprehend these seven p's, you'll be well equipped with a knowledge base that will serve as a solid platform on which you can intelligently build your life. Knowledge is power. The more powerful you become, the greater threat you pose to Satan and his kingdom. More importantly, you'll dually become a most viable asset to the Kingdom of God. It is my prayer that you will take this knowledge that the Holy Spirit has revealed to me and pour it into others that you encounter along your spiritual journey.

One of my former pastors and mentors, Bishop Martha J. Thomas always reminded us that this life is about two things: living and giving. Giving is not always financial. When we give of our spiritual knowledge, we are perhaps using our greatest resource—it shall never be exhausted because it is divinely inspired. The Holy Spirit Himself is an inward well of water springing up into everlasting life (John 4:14). Jesus informed the woman of Samaria at the well that if she would drink of Him, she would never thirst again, and the same holds true for you and me. It's not so much that one sip will eternally keep us satisfied. Moreover, the water supply from which we drink will never run dry. And much like the 23rd Psalmist, we shall not want. How refreshing to have thirsted after righteousness and been filled. With that being said, I hope you're hungry. There is a bounty of p's awaiting consumption and digestion. Therefore, I charge you in the spirit of my dearly departed mother Rebecca that you not even think about leaving this spiritual table until your plate is clean.

CHAPTER TWO

Eat Your Praises
(The Black-eyed Pea)

T he first p we will consume and digest is praise. In this chapter, we are going to take an in-depth look into what praise is as well as the multifaceted manner in which praises can and should be rendered to our God. We shall also take into account its necessity as well as the uncharted, stratospheric realm of praise into which few have tapped.

As I previously confessed, eventually, all of the peas my father and grandfather grew managed to grow on me. And while I don't remember any specific order in which the gradual affinity took place, one thing is for sure, black-eyed peas were the first that I came to enjoy. I don't know if it was the house-filled smell of the savory smoked meat that Mama used to flavor the peas as they simmered on the stove, or perhaps it was a desire to be like Dad and partake in his excitement about traditionally eating black-eyed peas on New Year's Day. Regardless of the reason, I fell in love with black-eyed peas first.

Was praise one of the first things you fell in love with when you became a Christian? Had we realized the power encased therein, perhaps we would have delved deeper rather than striving to graduate from animated praise as if it's merely a pastime for novice believers. When God saves sinners, He gives each of them the fundamental tools they will need to become strong Christians, and there are deeply-rooted reasons why one of the first passions He bestows is praise. Whether your passion stemmed from a favorite Gospel tune that never seemed to get old or a loud and shameless shout of joy that you habitually rendered during worship service at a pitch that seemed to be your own unique decibel, I believe that all true Christians, at some point, enjoy praising the Lord. It matters not how charismatic your praise is, for God observes sincerity of heart rather than volume. However, those who feel the need to engage in a more physical demonstration of praise should never feel pressured to muffle it. The book of Psalms not only gives us options for praise but grants us permission while commanding everything to find a way to offer those unique praises to our deserving God.

> Praise ye the LORD
>
> Praise ye the LORD from the heavens;
> praise him in the heights.
> Praise ye him, all his angels:
> praise ye him, all his hosts.
> Praise ye him, sun and moon:
> praise him, all ye stars of light.
> Praise him, ye heavens of heavens,
> and ye waters that be above the heavens.

Let them praise the name of the LORD: for he commanded, and they were created. He hath also stab-
lished them for ever and ever: he hath made a decree
which shall not pass.

Praise the LORD from the earth,
ye dragons, and all deeps:
Fire, and hail; snow, and vapours;
stormy wind fulfilling his word:
Mountains, and all hills;
fruitful trees, and all cedars:
Beasts, and all cattle;
creeping things, and flying fowl:
Kings of the earth, and all people;
princes, and all judges of the earth:
Both young men, and maidens;
old men, and children:

Let them praise the name of the LORD:
for his name alone is excellent;
his glory is above the earth and heaven.
He also exalteth the horn of his people,
the praise of all his saints;
even of the children of Israel,
a people near unto him.

Praise ye the LORD. (Psalm 148)

Praise ye the LORD. Sing unto the LORD a new
song, and his praise in the congregation of saints.

Let Israel rejoice in him that made him: let the children
of Zion be joyful in their King.

Let them praise his name in the dance: let them sing praises unto him with the timbrel and harp.

For the LORD taketh pleasure in his people: he will beautify the meek with salvation.

Let the saints be joyful in glory: let them sing aloud upon their beds. (Psalm 149:1-5)

Praise ye the LORD. Praise God in his sanctuary: praise him in the firmament of his power.

Praise him for his mighty acts: praise him according to his excellent greatness.

Praise him with the sound of the trumpet: praise him with the psaltery and harp.

Praise him with the timbrel and dance: praise him with stringed instruments and organs.

Praise him upon the loud cymbals: praise him upon the high sounding cymbals.

Let every thing that hath breath praise the LORD. Praise ye the LORD. (Psalm 150)

Having so many options makes it easy to be you and still offer appropriate praises. The goal is to become more concerned about the FACT of praise than the STYLE of praise. We were commanded to praise God and it is not optional. If you happen to have a more reserved personality, don't let someone else's eye-catching style cause you to shun the aspect of praise itself. The act of praise is vital to your spiritual connection with God and should be engaged on a daily basis. That's right. Praise is not just a weekly church event. Private praise can be just as powerful as corporate praise.

Let us explore what praise actually is. Praise has been reduced by many to enthusiastic clapping, singing, and dancing to loud music. Does that suggest that if one doesn't attend a feisty church that lends itself to such activity, he doesn't properly praise God? Failure to understand the complexity of praise could lead the narrow-minded believer down such a path. While animated praise plays a key role, I dare say that many have worked up a good sweat and still failed to offer meaningful and acceptable praises.

When a new convert has accepted Christ as his Savior and embarks upon his walk with the Lord, there are certain things he is typically taught, such as how to read the Bible, how to pray, how to become an active church member, and how to tithe. Yet, too often we fail to teach the fresh believer the vital skill of praising God. A most simple definition of praise is an expression of admiration, approval, and gratitude to God. How can something so simple be so powerful? Remember, how I stated earlier that God is a spirit? His very being is always fully spiritual. Therefore, God has to tap into our praises emotionally. It's spiritual for Him and should be spiritual for us as well. Do you say "hallelujah" because you've been asked to or because you've been taught that it's a cool praise word to be chosen? Instead, try focusing on something specific that God has done for you prior to uttering a word of praise. As you begin to feel the emotions of gratitude and joy flooding your soul, allow your hallelujah to be an expression that is offered as a result of what you feel. Now you're giving God (a spiritual being) something that He can feel. Get this equation in your heart and remember it always:

Purpose + Praise = Power

> Oh that men would praise the Lord for his goodness,
> and for his wonderful works to the children of men!
> (Psalm 107:8)

> Bless the LORD, O my soul, and forget not all his benefits:
> Who forgiveth all thine iniquities; who healeth all thy diseases;
> Who redeemeth thy life from destruction;
> who crowneth thee with lovingkindness and tender mercies;
> Who satisfieth thy mouth with good things; so that
> thy youth is renewed like the eagle's. (Psalm 103:2-5)

My father took great pride in his gardening. Daily, I was tasked to accompany him after he got off work and walk over to the garden to help him work some more. Any fresh weeds that had sprouted, we would up-root by hoe and hand. In an effort to keep things as organic as possible, Dad strove to avoid pesticides. This meant that any bugs that were munching on our potential harvest were diverted or thumped away. My father would till the ground to aerate the roots. If any plant growth appeared to be thwarted, he would use natural fertilizers. The days and seasons were monitored to ensure proper planting in cooperation with nature that the most bountiful harvest might be made possible. We would even pray for God to bless, protect, and cultivate the garden that it might bring forth awesome vegetation. Why so much fuss? Why such labor? Why not just plant it and forget it? Sorry to disappoint you, but there's no big philosophical explanation behind this dissertation. My father simply loved his family and wanted us to have the best. Do you love God so much that you want Him to have the best? Do you feel He's worthy of such? What does your best praise "look" like? Are you trying to perfect it? Do you ever challenge yourself to at least give God a better praise or do you simply plant your praise and forget it?

The longest book of the Bible is The Book of Psalms. Evidently, praise is of great importance to God. He inhabits, which means He lives in our praises (Psalm 22:3). He is God and He can choose to dwell just about anywhere. Yet, He chooses to inhabit our praises? Yes. Praise is His dwelling place of choice. If you could build a residence for God, how big would it be? Would you be embarrassed to make it too big out of concern for what others might think? When you are stingy with your praise, you are offering an amazing God a shack to live in. If I owned a shack and God was coming over to stay for a while, I'd at least try to make some home improvements or try to scrape together enough money to put Him in a hotel. But if I know God, He'd be just fine in my shack if that's the best I have to offer. However, if I had a mansion around the corner and put God in the shack, it wouldn't sit too well with Him because He's a jealous God. I believe this scenario connotes what God feels like when we let Him live in our shacks of praise but give mansion praises at football games and at our kids' dance recitals. I hope you'll agree that the least we can do is give God equal praise and perhaps one day, we'll mature enough spiritually that we'll give him the best because the best is what He deserves.

This concept of praise invoking the presence of God further suggests that the intensity and spirituality of our praise could determine the weight of the anointing each believer will experience in his or her lifetime.

Much praise = Much power

Less praise = Less power

No praise = No power

Keep in mind that power is authority. It is the ability to get things done. How on earth do you expect to have authority and get things done without a strong presence of God in your life?

> And at midnight Paul and Silas prayed, and sang praises unto God: and the prisoners heard them. And suddenly there was a great earthquake, so that the foundations of the prison were shaken: and immediately all the doors were opened, and every one's bands were loosed. (Acts 16:25-26)

We will now examine various types of "praisers," if you will. Praiser is not a word per the Cambridge Dictionary, and I was floored when I learned this fact. However, there are some that acknowledge it as the noun form of praise. Defiant as it may be, I am going to utilize the term "praiser" in this book, and we will consider it spiritual terminology for one who praises. On our Christian journey, we are endeavoring to adopt praise as a lifestyle, and if that doesn't make us praisers, then I don't know what else you're going to call us. I pray that this passage will influence and transform so many Christians into self-professed praisers that the word will have to be added to all official dictionaries across the globe. And, whether that happens or not, today I have chosen to exercise my right to freedom of speech and vow to wear the title of praiser 'til the day I die. Hallelujah!

THE OPTIONAL PRAISER is one who views praise as an elective rather than a prerequisite. I cannot stress to you enough that we are commanded to praise God. Even everything in nature brings praises to God. How can this be? How can an inanimate object offer praise? Remember we earlier learned that a spiritual connotation must be attached as praise is bestowed upon the Lord God Almighty. So, the fact that nature executes all of its duties in obedience to God's divine will brings great intangibles such as satisfaction, glory, honor and praise to Him on a regular basis. They praise Him by doing exactly what they are supposed to do and being exactly what they were created to be. Needless to conclude, it is not optional for the Christian to regularly be found doing exactly as God desires. Therefore Christians who fail to observe the necessary consistencies of praise are optional praisers and that is not a category into which we should fall.

Are you one of those church members who sits with a smile of approval plastered on his face while watching others actively engage in praise? Has Satan deceived you into believing that it's "okay" for you to NOT praise God? When the Holy Spirit is reigning and ruling within you, not too much time can elapse before He demands praise.

> Sing unto the Lord, praise ye the Lord: for he hath delivered the soul of the poor from the hand of evildoers. (Jeremiah 20:13)

> O praise the Lord, all ye nations: praise him, all ye people. For his merciful kindness is great toward us: and the truth of the Lord endureth for ever. Praise ye the Lord. (Psalm 117)

If *they rest neither day nor night* in heaven from giving God praises (Revelation 4:8), and we are not pleased to praise Him here on the earth, what do we think we're going to be doing when we get into heaven? I doubt that there will be a section in the rear for people to sit with a smile plastered on their faces while watching the rest of us praise God. I suppose it's possible, but given the fact that heaven is a place of sacred unity, I feel confident that we will be walking by the same rules and minding the same things. As you read through the book of Revelation you'll find that when praises were uttered from heaven, the author had no problem articulating to us what was being exclaimed because everyone was synchronizing their praises. Heaven is a place of matchless order orchestrated by the power of the Holy Ghost. While on earth we enjoy the freedom of individuality and choices as a part of the liberty given to mankind upon creation. However, once we receive our glorified bodies and reign with God as spiritual beings, it could be that a new spiritual cadence will manifest itself. I shudder to think of the amazing outpouring of God's power that we would experience if such unity were routinely achieved when congregations offer God praises here on earth.

Now that you have come into the knowledge of the necessity of praise, begin disciplining yourself in an effort to adopt praise as a lifestyle. Try incorporating facets of praise into your daily activities. Strive to ponder the things for which you are grateful to God and immediately offer Him praise for them. Find fresh and innovative ways to praise. The possibilities are endless. Pausing to offer God a prayer of thanksgiving is a means of giving Him praise. Living a devoted life free from iniquity brings Him praise. Obedience to His Word, submission to His will and yielding to the lead of His Holy Spirit each serves to bring God praise. Understand that offering an act of praise is beautiful but is also temporary. Living a lifestyle of praise is equally as beautiful but is perpetual. Think of how much more glorious our temporary acts of praise would be if our lifestyles preluded them.

THE IGNORANT PRAISER, who is perhaps the most common type of praiser, is one who praises God out of habit and/or without focus. He praises for personal or social gratification rather than seeking to gratify God, perhaps rarely considering if his acts of praise are even acceptable to God; much less pleasing to Him. The ignorant praiser doesn't take praise very seriously and therefore offers praise as a means of eye and lip service instead of solely to the Lord. If you have been guilty of being an ignorant praiser you must strive to get to the root of why in order to change. If you fail to deal with the root of this problem, you could fool yourself into thinking you can eradicate this behavior when you get ready. However, this problem is less behavioral and more spiritual. Ask yourself: What is hindering my focus and why do I allow it to do so? Why am I unconcerned about whether or not my praise gratifies the God whom I serve? I challenge you to examine the status of your relationship with Him. The deeper your relationship is with God, the more prone you will be to seek to please Him with every aspect of your spiritual walk, including praise. The goal is for your relationship to reach a level of intensity that demands quality praise. A spirit of mediocrity could be lurking. God would rather you be hot or cold. Lukewarm praisers will be spewed out of His mouth (Revelation 3:14-16). What a gruesome reality to learn that decades of habitual praises have been rejected by the one to whom they were offered.

THE DELIBERATE PRAISER attempts to use praise, prayer, and church attendance as tools to get what he wants out of God. This praiser always has a desired end result in mind, behaves like a spoiled child, and performs only to manipulate God into doing what he wants done. Should God mercifully grant his desired petition, he will resort back to a nearly praise-free lifestyle until his next need arises. Often, out of guilt, the deliberate praiser will be found praising God on special occasions in an effort to make up for lost time. This praiser feels obligated to bring an especially high praise to celebrate Resurrection Day or during revival services. Moreover, after having engaged himself in anti-Christian-like activities throughout the week, you can't beat the deliberate praiser squaring his situation with God by singing and shouting on Sunday mornings.

The saddest aspect of this category is that deliberate praisers often live as beneficiaries of God's grace. He showers it on them as a result of His merciful kindness. However, they confuse this to mean that their service has been acceptable unto Him.

Satan has deceived many of us in to believing that when things are going well, we must be alright with God. And when things are going poorly, we must be doing something wrong. Both theories could be far from the truth. Scripture bears out the fact that God rains on the just as well as the unjust (Matthew 5:44-46). This means God doesn't have tiny clouds reserved to hover over your house and water your lawn because you're holy and leave your neighbor's lawn to turn brown and burn under the scorching sun if your neighbor is a sinner. We all benefit from His love, mercy, and grace. Other than Jesus Christ, what better example have we biblically than that of Job to teach us that we can suffer afflictions although we may have done nothing to warrant them (Job 1:1-19)? Let us stop cheating ourselves out of manifold blessings by settling for below averageness because we're somewhat blessed. Why not seek for the blessings that God promised to pour out, and we wouldn't have room enough to receive them? Most of us have always had plenty of room to receive all with which God has blessed us. This means that there are higher heights we can attain. Deliberate praise is a level that may garner a few benefits. But if we desire more, let's do more (Malachi 3:9-11).

THE SPORADIC PRAISER understands the sanctity of praise and well knows what it is to experience blessings and thereafter offer sincere praises to God. However, this praiser makes the mistake of allowing outer entities to influence his spiritual will. Having such a weakness results in praises that are predicated on feelings and circumstances rather than on obedience to the Word of God. This is the praiser who will arrive early to church and rejoice nearly the entire service because God intervened on his job, and he avoided a layoff. But two weeks later, when a thunderstorm has caused a tree limb to fall and damage his car, he is too bitter to come to church and praise God. If he's not feeling it, it won't happen.

Well, at least sporadic praisers are sincere about their praises. But they often allow Satan to cheat them out of receiving the elite category of blessings reserved for those who praise God in spite of what's going on in their lives (1 Thessalonians 5:18). Sporadic praisers would do well to learn the lesson David did when he finally saw the need to offer sacrifices of joy and praises to God even while his enemies had risen up against him (Psalm 27).

Learn to stabilize your praise. Consistency (faithfulness) moves God. Taking the time to fully learn and understand God, your creator and source of everything, and living your life accordingly will help out in this area. Consider the kind of employee who is deemed a "good employee" by the boss. After this employee has proven himself, the boss eventually identifies the employee as being one on whom he can depend. This means the employee should consistently perform at a high level whether in or out of the boss' presence, when the workload is heavy, and even pick up the slack of coworkers without complaint. Can God depend on your praises? Will your praise waver from season to season? During church services, are you one who will pick up the slack of others to ensure that God receives adequate praise as you enter into His presence?

Let me encourage you to proactively eradicate every sporadic spirit that threatens your praise. Only the proactive Christians will escape this realm, for it is human nature to react based on how we feel. But, when we learn to praise God in spite of how we feel and without regard to the circumstances surrounding us, we break through into yet another special realm of blessings. God has special blessings reserved for the persevering saints (Revelation 3:11-12). There is a blessing in pressing. This prize is of the *high calling* of God and few will come to find it (Philippians 3:14-15).

THE PRIVATE PRAISER values his walk with God but confines his praises to the home and/or church setting. This praiser is ashamed to let his light shine before men and tries to blend in with sinners in the work place, in school, and in social settings. It is far more important for him to be accepted among his peer group than for his praises to be consistently acceptable to God. This praiser will even go as far as to suppress praises during worship services if unyielding visitors or critical, unsaved friends are present.

Private praisers are uncomfortable with living a lifestyle of praise. It was only engaged by them because it seemed socially acceptable at the time. Without realizing it, they have allowed a spirit of shame to overpower their will. But, this is the time that the praiser should engage in radical praises which will render the enemy powerless against the power of praise. Mind you, Satan realizes that he is powerless against the authority of believers when they praise. Therefore, his only shot at dismemberment is breaking the unity of the praisers. If he can deter one, the chain is broken. This doesn't mean that God will not accept the praises of the faithful few. But, it could mean the miracle-working realm that may have been reached through total unity is less accessible. Remember that Jesus said he would be ashamed to own us before his Father which is in heaven if we were ashamed to own him before men (Matthew 10:32-33). Our access to God is through Jesus. Private praisers stifle the pleasure of Jesus to ask God to execute miracles on our behalf. He becomes ashamed of us because we are ashamed of Him. Before we too quickly dismiss the accusation of us being ashamed, we should ask ourselves if our actions are speaking louder than our words. Praise should go to another level in the presence of unbelievers, scoffers, and doubters. We should be the prevailing force in every circumstance because of the authoritative power that works within. Let us transform every atmosphere with our praises as we unashamedly own God before men. In so doing, we will cause them to glorify the "Father which is in heaven" (Matthew 5:16).

SEVEN MORE REASONS WHY YOU SHOULD EAT THE BLACK-EYED PEAS OF PRAISE:

1. Black-eyed peas are styled as the heat-loving crop. When things become heated in your life, turn up the praises. They are guaranteed to thrive under heated conditions.

2. We already know that peas improve the quality of the soil in which they are grown. While studying the black-eyed peas, it was George Washington Carver who discovered that they were adding nitrogen to the soil in which they were planted. When you adopt a lifestyle of praise, the problems of this life will seem small. This repetitive escape into the spirit realm will improve your overall quality of life by relieving stress, abandoning thoughts of depression, and reconditioning your overall spiritual well-being.

3. Black-eyed peas are considered a soul food. The secular artists known as "The Black Eyed Peas" adopted the name because it sounded soulful like their music. From now on, think of praise as food for your soul.

4. Black-eyed peas are considered to be a symbol of prosperity because of how they swell when they are cooked. In hopes of a prosperous New Year, many Americans traditionally consume black-eyed peas. Also, many churches are adopting a tradition held by American churches of African American descent since The Emancipation Proclamation on 1/1/1863 to have a Watch Night service on New Year's Eve to bring in the New Year together, serving the Lord. What better way to ensure a prosperous year than praising God in unity with your brothers and sisters at the onset?

5. The first domestication of black-eyed peas is believed to have been on the continents of Africa and Asia before spreading throughout the world. Biblical historians have

taught us that human life also began on the continent of Africa before spreading throughout the world. Therefore, it wouldn't be farfetched to believe that the first praises to God were uttered from this same continent and those praises have spread throughout the world.

6. During the Civil War, black-eyed peas were considered an animal food. Therefore, when the union raided the confederate's food supply, they left these peas behind for the animals to eat and many confederates survived on black-eyed peas. They viewed themselves "lucky" to have them. When the enemy comes in and steals everything from you, understand that he cannot steal your praise. He is forced to leave it behind. That which he left will become your survival lifeline to heaven.

7. Black-eyed peas, without lengthy soaking, can be cooked quicker than other similar peas. How long does it take you to cook up a hot praise from the depths of your soul? Would you believe I've encountered many individuals who take pride in the fact that it takes a spiritual tidal wave of tsunami proportion for them to feel the Sprit and rejoice during a church service? What happened to the days of only having to think of the goodness of Jesus for a Christian to become overwhelmed? How can we be a light to the dark world if we allow our outward expressions to God to be haphazard and rare? God desires that we be lively stones for Him (1 Peter 2:5). Our God is a consuming fire (Hebrews 12:29). Don't be the type of Christian who has to *catch* on fire. Strive to be on fire for God at all times.

Here are seven songs I recommend for your meditation and focus regarding praise:

"There's a Story Behind My Praise" by Carolyn Taylor

"You Deserve It" by J.J. Hairston & Youthful Praise

"Praise the Lord" by Chris Christian

"O Praise the Name (Anastasis)" by Hillsong Worship

"That Name" by Yolanda Adams

"I Just Want to Praise You" by Maurette Brown Clark

"Praise the Father, Praise the Son" by Chris Tomlin

CHAPTER THREE

Eat Your Purging
(The Chickpea)

In this chapter we will learn the importance of purging the
soul. We will learn that purging is a dual process in which
God engages the believer's ability to lay aside some things and
offers His divine insight regarding which things may require His
assistance to excrete. By the end of this chapter, you should have
thorough knowledge of why this process is ongoing for all growing
Christians and is a crucial component of spiritual success.

Chickpeas are unique in that they assist the body with two important functions. They are high in dietary fiber. Fiber aids the
body with the process of eliminating wastes, toxins, and all of
the stuff we don't need. Ironically, chickpeas are also high in protein. In fact, they're just a little higher in protein than they are in

fiber. So, as badly as the chickpea desires to help you get rid of everything you don't need, it's even more concerned with helping you to build your muscles which will give you the strength you'll need to thrive. How healthy is a body that is filled with big muscles but layered through and through with just as much fat? That body would have a hard time using those wonderful muscles because the excess fat would weigh the body down causing it to be lethargic or easily exhausted. Have you ever encountered an individual who frequently works out at the gym but can't seem to get rid of the fat around their abdomen? Believe it or not, many of these people already have washboard abs but can't see them because they are covered by that layer of abdominal fat. If they could purge their bodies of that abdominal fat, perhaps they would recognize how strong they actually are. But, few people are willing to adhere to a strict diet thus undergoing the strenuous elimination process which is a necessary supplement to the exercising they have been doing. How depressing to know that the hard work in which they've been engaged may never be appreciated by others because the evidence is concealed. All anyone can see is the fat.

Purge means to get rid of whatever is impure or undesirable. If you are a new Christian, please begin the process of purging early in your walk with God. Learn to lay aside the weight and the sin that can so easily beset you. If you do so, you'll be able to run the race with patience that God has set before you (Hebrews 12:1). Patient runners are able to enjoy the process of running. God wants you to enjoy your journey. But carrying too much excess baggage will make your journey harder than it has to be. Come out from among people that are anti-Christian and live a lifestyle that is separate from them (2 Corinthians 6:17). Embrace holiness by quickly freeing yourself from anything that threatens your walk with God.

I used to work in downtown Nashville. Like in most metropolitan downtown areas, I had to do quite a bit of walking to get to the office each day. Often, I would encounter the same bustling people as I was making my way to work. I would sometimes see one man in particular who was unlike the others. He wasn't wearing a business suit. He had no plush office inside one of the skyscrapers. He was homeless. However, there was something different about this man. I noticed that he didn't sit idly as did many of the other homeless individuals. He was often carrying a long narrow stick and would rhythmically march up and down the street with no shirt on. He seemed proud of his chiseled physique and had salt and pepper dreadlocks halfway down his back. He would have been most magnetic were it not for the fact that the annoying and intimidating gibberish he shouted caused many a gazer to jaywalk in fearful avoidance. For some reason, I wasn't particularly afraid of the man. I found him rather intriguing. I even tried greeting him once or twice, but he ignored me as if he were on a mission and dared not be deterred. I finally decided that he was fifty percent mentally challenged and fifty percent rude—thus I left the man alone.

One day I overheard a few co-workers describing the man's odd behavior and decided I would join the discussion to share my experiences. But, I was soon mortified after another co-worker rushed over to sharply interject words of knowledge to us all. I won't use his real name, but it wasn't his name that shifted my mode to pause. It was his title and the story that captivated me. We'll call him John Doe. I was informed that Doe was once an upstanding citizen in the community. He was a successful medical doctor who was well respected. He also was a family man with a beautiful wife and children. However, this was during a time when people who were of African American descent and living in the south were not well accepted by some Caucasian southerners as having achieved such successes against the odds and prior to the civil rights movement. To further complicate things, I understood that Dr. Doe happened to be an out-spoken individual. He wasn't afraid to go against the status quo.

One evening, Dr. Doe was in a local bar unwinding after a long day's work. He entered a bar of his choosing, although it wasn't on the predominantly black side of town. A group of Caucasians approached him and intentionally struck up a controversial discussion. As he was turned to one of them expressing his pointed opinions, the other slipped something into his drink. Ever since that night, Dr. Doe has never been the same mentally. Needless to say, he could no longer practice medicine and somehow his neurotic behavior led to the dismantling of his once happy home. I don't exactly know how he spiraled down to homelessness, but I do now understand why this man, whom I regularly encountered, didn't seem as though he belonged on the street. He was a victim frantically seeking help, but he didn't have the mental capacity to request it. He was being tormented by a need for restoration to a place that he could no longer describe and perhaps restitution for all he had wrongfully lost.

I never looked at Dr. John Doe quite the same again, and the next time I saw him, something inside of me wanted to rescue him, but I didn't know how. I was also told that he went to many doctors, but each could do nothing to cure him. The damage had already taken a permanent toll. However, I had a hard time accepting such a stagnant prognosis. Was there no way to purge him of those toxins he'd ingested? Was there no psychiatrist who could purge his mind and restore him to his former state? He wouldn't stop and talk to me, so I don't know if he knows or ever knew Jesus, but the least I could do was remember him in prayer. For whether he knew it or not, he needed a purging that only God could provide.

At that very moment, I learned a life-lesson and subsequently tried to stop judging people by how they appeared. For, there is more to each of us than meets the eye. There is greatness inside of each of us.

We can't always see the greatness, but it's there. Sometimes it's buried so deeply that only God the Holy Ghost can reach far enough to bring about the resurrection. Sometimes, that greatness gets smothered as a result of self-inflicted layers of unneeded fat, such as addictions we initiate or sexually promiscuous voyages we take that yield habits so spiritually fattening, we wish we'd never taken them. Other times, greatness is subdued as a result of psychological damage we didn't choose – much like that of Dr. Doe. And yet the damage seems irreversible, like the suffering of molestation as an innocent minor or enduring the manifestation of a genetic disease such as multiple sclerosis or sickle cell anemia. Regardless of the origin or whom/what we feel is to blame, some things seemingly cannot be thoroughly uprooted without divine intervention. This realization is when God's purging process becomes empowered to commence.

The word "purge" also means to rid someone of an unwanted feeling, memory or condition. And wouldn't it be great if God's process of purging were just that simple? If He would reach down from glory and snatch out everything that's not like Him, leaving us flawless and ready to float away to heaven, we'd all be model Christians in deed. But God's ways are as far from ours as heaven is from earth (Isaiah 55:7-9). He doesn't think like we do. Therefore, in this chapter, we'll only be able to offer a glimpse into the bounty of reasons God may choose to do what He does; the way He does it. And what we don't know we'll be encouraged to accept by faith after we choke down a few of these spiritual chickpeas.

My parents exposed us to more than one facet of Christianity as we were growing up because they attended two different churches. Yet the principles they taught us at home were firm. Therefore, we didn't grow up confused about God and what He requires. We learned that we should live right both in and out of the confines of a sanctuary. Otherwise, we will be lost, even though our name is on a church's roll. It's funny how learning things as a child doesn't mean you won't stray, explore or even become defiant. But it does further sensitize your conscience. You are fully aware that what you are doing is wrong. And when you're ready to repent, the road back home is a lot shorter because you know the way.

Dad took us to the Christian Methodist Episcopal church across the street from our country-suburban home. Mom took us to the Pentecostal Holiness church in the hood, about a twenty-minute drive into North Nashville. These two churches were different in a lot of ways but had similarities as well.

When it came to purging the spiritually undesirable things, the church across the street fostered a loving and safe environment. They were consistently accepting of people regardless of their issues. They focused on drawing individuals through loving kindness. Once an individual made his mind up to give his heart to the Lord, the church across the street expected that He (God) would make the necessary changes in their lives. That church taught us right from wrong. But the atmosphere was never one that caused us to feel judged or as if we weren't welcomed although we had flaws and short comings.

The Pentecostal Holiness church in the hood took a more aggressive approach to purging impurities. They seemed to focus on intentionally pointing out the sins and shortcomings of others in an effort to expose the enemy and put him to flight. They didn't sugarcoat, and they didn't pacify. Tough love was their banner and they believed that the Word of God was going to either draw you or drive you. They styled the church as a hospital and would say that there is no point in coming to church one way and leaving the same.

As I grew up, I saw great successes in both churches:

I grew up in the neighborhood with some of the people who went to the Methodist church across the street. Some of them were engaged in sinful activities in which we weren't allowed to participate. But once they made up their minds, I saw them make solid changes and grow up to hold important offices in the church. They took those offices seriously. To this day, many of them are still executing their devotion to God with the utmost integrity. I've seen my peers become great role models, assume the important position of stewardship, and some have even accepted a calling into the ministry. I am so proud to have witnessed these miraculous transformations. Whenever I go back to my home church to visit, it does my heart good. Sometimes I'm even moved to tears, and I am encouraged to see evidence of the fact that God is a life-transforming God who is true to the promises in His Word.

In the Pentecostal Holiness church that was in the hood in North Nashville, I saw people come in off of the street who were visibly intoxicated. The Word of God would be preached to them. As a result, they would come to the altar and God would physically purge them as they cried out to Him for salvation and deliverance. I know many people who yet hold testimonies of instant deliverance from addictions such as cigarette smoking, crack cocaine, and alcoholism once they heard the Word of God and were filled with the Holy Ghost. Many became deacons, missionaries, evangelists, and ministers as well. I've seen God instantly bestow divine healing through the laying on of hands in powerful worship services, and I learned through firsthand experience the extent to which God will work miracles through the amazing power of faith.

As I grew up, I saw great failures in both churches:

Some people felt they were never challenged enough in the church across the street to make serious changes in their lives. Therefore, they left their home church and found the challenge they sought elsewhere. Some were never delivered from their addictions and left the church only to fall deeper into iniquity and have yet to find their way back to God. Others still attend church and sit in hypocrisy knowing they need change but seem somehow relieved by the fact that no one is badgering them about it. People are just glad they are still coming.

The church in the hood saw a mass exodus of young people who were tired of feeling browbeaten about what they shouldn't do instead of being motivated to do more. They found churches that celebrated and appreciated their gifts and they began to flourish there. Others went off to college and rebelled against what they were taught with zero intentions of returning. There were also those who buckled beneath the peer pressure-like atmosphere of the church and became great pretenders who danced and spoke in tongues in front of the congregation on Sunday but were caught up in Pentecostal no-no's outside of the sanctuary such as clubbing, fornication, and homosexuality.

I am not someone who is on the outside pointing a finger at what I think takes place in other churches. I personally experienced these atmospheres for many years. Because I saw great successes and great failures in both churches, I can comprehensively conclude that there is not one religious method that works for all people. This was addressed in the book of Jude:

> Keep yourselves in the love of God, looking for the mercy of our Lord Jesus Christ unto eternal life. And of some have compassion, making a difference: And others save with fear, pulling them out of the fire; hating even the garment spotted by the flesh. (Jude 21-23)

Each of us is uniquely designed with varying personalities, needs, feelings and levels of faith. Therefore, God himself must design a purging process that is in our individual best interest. Much like the chickpea, His process will purge with spiritual fiber and, at the same time, build muscle with spiritual protein. It is vitally important that we engage God in the specific purging process He selects and allow patience to "have her perfect work" (James 1:4). For only God knows what it will take to purge us, how many layers we have that need to be cut away and how the properly-timed purging sessions must be strategically planned else we could risk permanent damage that will yield death rather than life. We don't have to like it, but we do have to accept it if we desire paramount spiritual success.

Let's examine some of the magnificent purging concepts of God that take place in the spirit realm through our life experiences. God strategically purges His people using either of the concepts mentioned in the book of Jude when applicable. If we dare attempt to aid a wayward soul in this supernatural procedure, each concept is critical and must be chosen wisely. There is a demonic world full of evil spirits and they can influence our behaviors. Cancelling out the authority that these spirits have in our lives is the purging that many of us desperately need. And unfortunately, that includes the saved as well as the unsaved. We'll get back to that a little later in this chapter.

I don't know why many religious denominations feel that they have the monopoly on the best ways to do everything. I feel that if we spent more time learning from each other rather than judging each other, we could get a lot more accomplished for God. But for some reason, religion and politics are two subjects that people might be willing to discuss but rarely are open enough to change their minds regarding. This is why I am so excited to be living in the twenty first century. The Millennial Generation is not so locked into the traditional concepts of how to do things.

They are readily open to change and are consistently searching for modern methods that are quicker, smarter, and more efficient.

Since we've brought up Millennials, let's deal with younger people for a moment as many churches are struggling to retain individuals who fall into this age bracket. In order to be successful in loosening the grip that Satan has on many within this youthful generation, we must first accept the fact that what worked for our generation may not work for theirs. Just as God knows better than to give precious pearls to swine, He cannot give us the precious answers we need if we are so close-minded to new things that we ignore their value (Matthew 7:6). God said, "Behold, I will do a new thing..." (Isaiah 43:19) How dare the body of Christ tell God that they neither want nor need anything new? My Dad taught me to be careful not to waste too much time on plan A. Once you see it's not working, move to plan B. Furthermore, make sure you always have a plan B. Don't sit there and watch plan A empty all of your pews before you'll entertain another concept. Seek guidance through the Holy Spirit regarding which purging method He has ordained to be used to help each soul and let Him do His work.

It's unrealistic to expect any one church to save everybody. However, as Christians, we must expect God to save and deliver everybody who comes to Him. He's more than able to do so. We constrict the omnidirectional ability He has when we as vessels offer Him a tunnel vision mindset with which to work. I can't help but wonder what might have happened had both of the churches to which I was exposed embraced a multilayered purging concept according to the book of Jude. What if they'd both diagnosed personalities and catered to the individual needs of their congregants? When we clearly perceive that a system is failing, we should immediately make a change. If the change attempt fails, we've lost nothing additional. The original plan was already failing. Reverend Brenda Moss was the first individual I ever heard use the phrase, "Nothing beats a failure but a try." She and I worked together in a congregation for several years. I was a young minister, and I don't recall exactly what my dilemma was, but I'll never forget how it felt as she used the power of her tongue to chase away all of my hesitations with that one sentence. Too often we base our future on the failures of our past as if God is an inconsequential bystander, powerless to intervene. Knowing who God is should be breeding ground enough to bring forth the courage we need to admit our failures and confidently try again.

> But without faith it is impossible to please him: for he that cometh to God must believe that he is, and that he is a rewarder of them that diligently seek him. (Hebrews 11:6)

I've talked a lot about helping others. But, God also wants to help you. While it may be true that the churches to which I was exposed should have diversified their tactics, it's equally true that the church goers who were in need of purging should have been spiritually mature enough to look beyond the method and see the love. Both churches meant well. That's why this book needs to get into the hands of new converts. If new converts can grasp the concept of purging early enough, they'll become so stable and mature that they won't waver throughout the process even if it comes via a method they don't particularly enjoy. Naaman didn't particularly enjoy having to dip himself seven times into the muddy Jordan River. But, his desire to be healed from the incurable disease of leprosy far outweighed his foolish pride that could have cost him his life had he not overcome it. Pray for the spirit of Naaman to sweep over the body of Christ that it might help to save this wayward generation (2 Kings 5:1-15).

Against the odds, I got married at age nineteen with no money and no job. Most of the people in my life, as well as in my wife's family, thought we were crazy. Some even predicted failure. But, they didn't know that God had clearly instructed both of us that this was what we needed to do. Had we not done so, fleshly desires would have consumed us. Because we obeyed God, He quickly blessed us both with stable employment. A few months after my twentieth birthday, we became homeowners. I wish I could tell you that the marriage was lovely and life has been sweet, but nothing could be further from the truth. It was an extremely difficult route to take and I would never recommend that anyone get married without stable sources of income. But the marriage itself and even the difficulties that came along with it were God's way of purging us from that which the enemy had designed to destroy us spiritually. We were young dating Christians who were playing with fire and didn't understand the power of those flames. Instead of God trying to explain all of that to us, He simply snatched us out. I have learned that when God rescues you from one of Satan's traps, it angers him, and he comes hard for you in other ways. He is relentless in his pursuit to kill, steal and destroy (John 10:10). Moreover, he doesn't play fair. And while I have been far from flawless as a husband, I have learned from my mistakes and the biggest proclamation I have is that, after over twenty-five years of trying, Satan has been unsuccessful at his mission to end our marriage.

I'll never forget my first job after getting married. It was for a small company not far from my home. I was so excited to be working for such a corporation that I worked circles around my colleagues and was later offered a supervisory role. The company was so small that I reported directly to the Vice President. But he was so busy running the technology department that I often answered directly to the CEO. The CEO was a stern and intimidating business man with a loud, booming voice. However, once you got to know him, he was of a gentle and kind spirit. He just had zero tolerance for foolishness and wasn't about to allow his business to fail as a result.

One morning, he called me into his office to offer me some sage advice with regard to my new role as a supervisor. He explained to me that a common mistake many managers make is locking into one management style. He said, "Take Ralph for example. I know I can call Ralph in here and chew his a_ _ and he will walk right out that door and work twice as hard. But if I call Judy in and try the same thing, she'll burst into tears and have to go home for the rest of the day. And God forbid I try that with Brenda. She'll snap right back and say, 'Who do you think you are? Nobody talks to me that way!' And poor sweet Leonard would quietly listen to every word without verbal retaliation but would eventually turn in his resignation, never explaining why. And then there's you, William. If I chew you out, I know you'll eventually find a way to tell me exactly how you feel as well. But, as long as I talk to you with some respect and show appreciation for your progress, I know you'll walk right out of my office and apply everything I tell you and continue to consistently work hard for me. You've got to learn the personalities of the people who work for you and give them what they need, so they will give you what you need." This is the same Judaic principle God revealed in His word. While I love the way Jude articulated it, he was not the originator of the concept. God began purging His chosen people in the same way not long after they left Egypt and found themselves in the wilderness. He saw the need to purge them from their slave mentality and teach them how to stand on their own two feet while trusting Him and Him only. Believe it or not, these newly-freed sojourners longed to return to slavery simply for the security they'd previously enjoyed. When they were slaves, they didn't have to wonder if or when they would eat. In the wilderness, they had to wait on God to feed them manna on a daily basis. Because they were unaccustomed to living by faith, they felt insecure and doubted God. But God forced them to endure the necessary hardships that they might learn to depend on Him in all things. Whenever you pray and ask God to increase your faith, expect Him to increase everything in your life that requires it. He is the *supreme* on-the-job trainer. If you live it, you will learn it.

My father was a civil engineer who landed a position with the Federal Government and bore the distinction of becoming the first African American manager for the Corps of Engineers. He landed this position through the grace of God in the south shortly after the heat of the civil rights movement. So, I don't have to tell you that he was not well received. Even his secretary, who happened to be Caucasian, cringed to work for him. Therefore, I was eager to get his advice in my new role. Dad's advice was similar to that of the CEO. Dad said, "The key to successful management is to find a way to get people to do what you want them to do. Not because they have to, but because they want to do it for you. If people care enough about you as a person that they want to work for you, you've got it made."

Dad spent a lot of time being genuinely nice to all of the people at his job, including the rude secretary, even though they weren't always nice to him. He tried to do right by people and live by the golden rule (Luke 6:31) regardless of the fact that people didn't always treat him the way they wanted to be treated. It took some time. Actually, it took a long time. But, Dad eventually won the respect and friendship of his Caucasian employees and colleagues alike. By the time he retired, they hated to see him go and many confessed that he was the best leader they'd ever had. Little did they know God used Dad to take them each through a purging process. God used Dad to purge them of prejudices and jealousies by forcing them to endure that which they wanted to avoid. Although they didn't like it initially, they were better off in the end.

While God is purging us, the enemy will whisper lies in an effort to convince us that God doesn't love us or is somehow punishing us and that's why we are going through trials. So, in order to dismantle the enemy's theory, we must elevate our thinking to a spiritual level.

> Finally, brethren, whatsoever things are true, whatsoever things are honest, whatsoever things are just, whatsoever things are pure, whatsoever things are lovely, whatsoever things are of good report; if there be any virtue, and if there be any praise, think on these things. (Philippians 4:8)

One of God's more drastic methods is to allow us to fall deeper into a situation that we are trying to get out of rather than to immediately snatch us out. With this method, God strategically takes his time when purging us. While God did supply the needs of the children of Israel, he left them in the wilderness for forty years. They should have only been there for forty days, but they needed to be purged. They were doubtful. They were chronic complainers. They longed to be like other nations rather than embracing who God created them to be. Sound familiar? These are the same issues that plague many Christians today. It is important to God that we develop an appreciation for His deliverance. God worked many miracles for the children of Israel, but they morphed into spoiled brats who seemed to only call on Him when they needed Him rather than serve Him humbly and loyally through an appreciative heart. Had they appreciated God, they would have been more consistently obedient to His will. It's not enough to love God for what He does. We should learn to love Him for whom He is. Deliverance has the power to draw us into this mindset of willful servitude when it's strategically granted. God doesn't just want you to be delivered. He wants you to develop an understanding of who He is and why He delivers. The deeper your appreciation, the greater your admiration can become for who God is, which can lead to a lifelong, loving relationship with Him.

God also does not want us to ever return to the thing from which he purges us. Scripturally, this is described as a dog returning to his own vomit. As grotesque and foolish as it sounds, too often we do it time and time again (Proverbs 26:11). As long as we believe God will bail us out, we keep committing crimes. Preachers don't like to teach this fact, but eventually, if we keep doing that, God will leave us sitting in spiritual prison without the possibility of parole. It's called being turned over to a reprobate mind—from which we cannot recover. He will see that you have made your choice to serve Satan and your conscience will no longer tap you on the shoulder to tell you that you should cease from what you are doing (Romans 1:28-32). I beg of you to humbly allow God to purge you of all your nasty habits and do not cleave to them.

> No man can serve two masters: for either he will hate the one, and love the other; or else he will hold to the one, and despise the other. Ye cannot serve God and mammon. (Matthew 6:24)

> And if it seem evil unto you to serve the Lord, choose you this day whom ye will serve; whether the gods which your fathers served that were on the other side of the flood, or the gods of the Amorites, in whose land ye dwell: but as for me and my house, we will serve the Lord. (Joshua 24:15)

> And Elijah came unto all the people, and said, How long halt ye between two opinions? if the Lord be God, follow him: but if Baal, then follow him. And the people answered him not a word. (1 Kings 18:21)

Do you remember the man who was born blind in the Bible? Jesus explained that his handicap was neither the result of his sin nor his parents' sin. The reason he was handicapped was so that God could one day deliver Him and be glorified for accomplishing the miraculous feat. How refreshing to know that even situations with which you've dealt all of your life could have been allowed so that one day, God can receive glory from having delivered you. It seems like an odd concept to grasp, but each of us is merely a lump of clay on the potter's wheel waiting to be formed into whatever God chooses to create. Some of us are ordained to have powerful testimonies of the things God brought us through. The generational curses, that have befallen us for things our forefathers did through which we suffer, don't necessarily come to break us. It could be that they have been allowed so that God can be honored once we are set free. If the woman with an issue of blood waited for twelve years, the lame man waited at the pool of Bethesda for thirty-eight years, the children of Israel waited in slavery for four hundred years, how long are you willing to wait until your purging is complete? You're going to wait. That choice is not up to you. The willingness to do so is what will determine how peaceful of a process you endure. It is entirely possible to bring glory to God in all that you do, including how you wait.

"Purge me with hyssop, and I shall be clean: wash me, and I shall be whiter than snow" (Psalm 51:7). The Psalmist is not requesting a cleansing agent that he feels is strong enough to clean him. He well knows that he needs a spiritual purging that only God can bring. However, he metaphorically dressed his request in the strongest cleanser known to man at that time. He did this to express to God the thoroughness that he desired. He wanted to be whiter than snow. How can you get any whiter than snow? I just wanted to give you a peek into the intensity of a prayer that got God's attention. Don't just tell God what to do. Explain to him the depth of purging that you need. Show him the sincerity behind your request.

Another reason God takes us through a purging process is because we were conceived in sin and shaped in iniquity. This means that our origin and everything that has been familiar to us from the time we were in our mother's womb is sin. It's all we know. It's how we think and it's how we govern our lives. We are conversant with it. Although we've always had a spirit, we have always lived by the flesh. Walking spiritually is new to us and it's going to take some getting used to. Consequently, if we ever hope to have a real chance at perfecting this spiritual walk, we need to be purged from the things that have controlled our mindset for so many years. Failure to do this can lead to a life of confusion and end in spiritual defeat. How many people do you know who started out as Christians and returned to their old ways? This happens because people fail to get completely purged from the world (carnality) and the things that are in it.

We have been taught scripturally to flee youthful lusts, to submit to God and resist the devil, to put off the carnal man, to mortify the deeds of the flesh, and so on. But all of these things are easier said than done. Therefore, we will round out this chapter by educating you on the spirit realm.

Satan (a.k.a. Lucifer) was a high-ranking angel before he was kicked out of heaven. When he decided to exalt his throne above God's throne, he had to go. But the Bible clearly states that he "took" those other stars with him (Revelation 12:4). I believe that those fallen angels became the evil spirits and demonic forces used by Satan to execute his evil will just as God uses heavenly angels to execute His divine will. That's the only way Satan knows to operate. It's how things operated where he came from and everything was perfect in heaven. He couldn't help but to structure his kingdom like God's and run it the same way. He's a product of his environment. I would dare say, it's the main reason he's been so dramatically successful. It was a smart strategy, and it has served him well.

Now, I know that God is all powerful, and if we have Him, we have power over the enemy. But, let's be realistic: If Satan was influential enough to draw a third of *heaven's host*, what makes you think you can just ignore him and be fine? Satan is going to come after you with both fists because you are now fighting on a different team. Remember, you were born in sin (on Satan's team) and basically, when you became a Christian, you betrayed him. You dumped him. You are now in love with his arch enemy, and he is not happy about that. He is going to try to draw you back to his team and understandably so. Therefore, you must understand how he works and completely detach from him along with everything that looks like and reminds you of him if you expect to successfully maintain your victorious deliverance. It sounds challenging because it is challenging. But, serious Christians must eventually face this challenge.

I'd like for you to accept the theory that God would never create a world that could potentially grow beyond His ability to manage it. So, if the two thirds of angels who are left in heaven execute God's will in heaven, manage his affairs on the earth and serve as guardians to each of us, there must be more angels and angelic beings than there are humans on the earth. The Bible says that Jesus could speak and twelve legions of angels would immediately come to take care of His needs (Matthew 26:53). A legion is the equivalent of a few thousand. The flip side is, the man who was possessed in the Bible and Jesus asked, "What is thy name?" The answer the demons gave was, "My name is legion: for we are many." (Mark 5:9) I don't think Satan is one to waste his time. So, if he can afford to permit a legion of angels to be inside of one man, it's logical to believe that even the fallen one-third of heaven greatly outnumbers us. Some commentators estimate that the demonic world outnumbers us a thousand to one. Based on what we've just explained, this estimation is realistic. I hope you're starting to understand why we are tempted all the day long to do evil and why it's always so easy to fall back into sin when we are not careful. Satan has enough agents that he can assign a separate evil spirit to you for every sinful weakness you have. And they have nothing better to do than follow you around all day and wait for opportunities to temp you to fall. And you think the Muslims are going overboard for committing to praying seven times a day? We need to be praying around the clock and all while we are asleep. It's no wonder that we lose so many spiritual battles. Our enemies are constantly strategizing and working to defeat us, while we only fight them when we are forced to defend ourselves.

Perhaps you're now wondering how hard we have to work to become and remain fully purged from all evils. My response is: I have no idea. But, I would suggest that you start by working as hard as you worked to get bound. Impress God with your zeal, fervor, and determination, so He'll be motivated to provide all of the help you will need. What makes us think that we can eat, sleep, and breathe sinful carnalities for decades and then say a sinner's prayer and expect to live a life of spiritual freedom? It simply doesn't work like that. We must fight the enemy and completely engage ourselves in spiritual warfare to become completely and successfully purged. Now, this is not for the mediocre Christians who are content to straddle the fence and believe that God is satisfied as long as our good deeds outweigh our bad. This is for the saints of God who want to see miracles work in their lives on a regular basis and who want to have some serious power in the spirit realm while being exponentially blessed beyond measure. Few will reach such a stratospheric spiritual level. But if I can educate your spirit man enough for you to realize that the spiritual status quo is not sufficient and motivate you to try harder, I guarantee you'll come out far better than you would have had you chosen to accept mediocrity. This requires a purged mindset. "Be ye transformed by the renewing of your mind" (Romans 12:2).

What do you aspire to become? Are you a Moses, a Joshua, or one of the children they led? Are you a Samson, a Deborah or one of the Israelites who celebrated their victories? Maybe you're a King like David. Or maybe you're just the doorkeeper whom great King David said he'd rather be. Perhaps you're an Apostle Peter, an Apostle Paul, or maybe you're more like one of the Christians they helped to become converted. There's room in heaven for each of the individuals in my analogies. But, to whom much is given, much is required. If you're reading this book, God wants you to tap into the greatness that is inside of you. Strive to become all that He has created you to be. Begin by purging yourself from any and everything that threatens your greatness, including your own insecurities, doubts, fears, apprehensions, prejudices, preconceived notions, past failures, and mental barriers.

As we conclude this chapter, here are three tips that will help you embrace God's purging process for your life and cause you to become an aid to the process.

1. **If it doesn't bring glory to God, question its necessity in your life.**

2. **Eat those spiritual chickpeas.** Every time you get rid of some unwanted spiritual fat, replace it with some spiritual, muscle-building protein. My father-in-law, Bishop Willie Walker, who is one of the most successful Apostles I ever encountered, was teaching this concept to freshly-delivered converts many years ago. He taught that if you decide to stop smoking, you need to create a healthy habit that will fill that void else the enemy will return and fill it for you. For example, many people smoke to relax. If that was the foundation for your habit, find something else to do that will relax you. The paramount decision would be

to choose something that also brings glory to God by edifying you spiritually. This is how you simultaneously build spiritual muscle. You may have to try several things until you find something that works for you, but it could be listening to your favorite genre of Gospel music, watching a religious-themed play production/movie, or curling up with a great book like *Eat Your Ps*!

3. **Openly testify about the changes that you have made in your life**. This reduces the likelihood of you going back to your old habits. It also builds accountability between you and those with whom you share it. If you inspired them, they'll need to hold on to that inspiration and they will not stand idly by and watch you fall.

SEVEN MORE REASONS WHY YOU SHOULD EAT THE CHICKPEAS OF PURGING:

1. Chickpeas have been identified as being shaped like a brain. This should remind us to think twice before we make a decision that might intercept God's purging process in our lives. If you're striving to live a Christian lifestyle, you're going to get purged now or later. Please, do it now. Trust the author. He speaks from experience and knows exactly what he's talking about.

2. While the chickpeas shown in the photo at the helm of this chapter are the most common in America, chickpeas come in other colors and flavors. However, their nutritional benefits remain consistent. If you're like me, you were sure there was only one kind of chickpea. Many people think they only have one main issue they'd like for God to help them get under control. But just like there are chickpeas we didn't know about, there are things about us that only God knows need to change. Let God purge you of

everything He deems necessary. You will consistently see spiritual benefits by doing so.

3. Dried chickpeas can be kept for an unlimited period of time. But once they have been soaked, they must be used within a couple of days. Satan loves for weights and sins to lie dormant within us indefinitely. But once God begins to soak us in the water we joyfully drew from the "wells of salvation" (Isaiah 12:3) our eyes will be opened to our hindrances through His word. At that point, we should quickly eradicate.

4. It is estimated that chickpeas were first cultivated in 7000 B.C. Isn't it satisfying to know that God provided the potential to purge us from our faults thousands of years before we even came to the knowledge of the necessity of such? There is nothing new under the sun. Seven thousand years later, Jesus was tempted just like we are. He just chose not to sin (Hebrews 4:15).

5. Chickpeas are most widely eaten in humble and poverty-stricken communities of Africa and Asia. It takes a great deal of humility to submit to purging. But, if you would humble yourself now under the mighty hand of God and eat your purging, He will exalt you in due time (1 Peter 5:6).

6. The flowers of the chickpea plant have the ability to self-pollinate. This means they will produce a harvest without any outside intervention. If God is purging you, He's all-sufficient and well-equipped to finish the job. And, when God finishes with us, we shall come forth shining like pure gold.

7. In one year, the life-cycle of the chickpea plant is complete. You may be experiencing the pangs of purging right now, but it won't always be like this.

Here are seven songs I recommend for your meditation and focus regarding purging:

"God Help Me" by Plumb

"Take It Away from Me" by Wilmington Chester Mass Choir

"A Heart That Forgives" by Kevin Levar

"Control" by Tenth Avenue North

"Make Me Over" by Tonex & The Peculiar People

"Fix Me" by Tim Bowman, Jr.

"Renew Me" by Martha Munizzi

CHAPTER FOUR

Eat Your Prayers (The Green Pea)

*I*n this chapter, we will endeavor to convey how vital and beneficial an active prayer life is to us as believers. We will also explore the different types of prayer and the various methods we can use to reach the same expected end. Prayerfully, (pun intended) by the end of this chapter, you will have an expanded perspective on prayer that will transform your prayer life into a joyful experience embraced by your spirit rather than a mundane ritual used only to satisfy selfish wants.

One of my wife's pet peeves is a one-sided telephone conversation. She hates for someone to call her and, following the greeting, just sit there holding the phone with nothing to say. She's wondering why they called in the first place and now she feels obligated to carry the conversation. She also hates when people dump information and are then ready to walk away. Being the detail diva that she is, she is rarely without additional questions. So, if you're going to start a conversation with her you'd better be prepared to finish it.

Simply stated, prayer is communication with God. Effective communication cannot take place unless both parties converse. Why then have we reduced prayer to a one-sided conversation? Are we guilty of contacting God with virtually nothing to say? Or do we merely dump our requests on God and then walk away? Are we guilty of starting a conversation with him but failing to block off time in case He has some things He'd like to say back to us?

Poor prayer habits are widely prevalent even among the most seasoned Christians. My good friend Chris Reid serves in The Church at Woodbine, a regional campus of the world-renowned Brentwood Baptist Church. While serving his church in a leadership capacity, he was charged with the task of praying for the needs of those within his group. Logically, he instituted a system by which each individual could submit their prayer needs to him, and he would avail himself in prayer on their behalf. After a long while of disciplining himself to pray, he began to notice prayer request patterns. Therefore, he compiled statistics for a period of one year and found some interesting results with regard to the prayer requests of Christians.

After he shared this data with me, I couldn't help but reflect on my more than twenty years as a fellow constituent of the clergy. The list was a striking replica of the prayer requests I've received and still do receive on a regular basis. I chose not to share the list, for I feel that God led my friend to conduct that research for a greater purpose that has yet to be revealed. But I will say that it was a bit painful to read the requests because they seemed rather selfish. I suppose it was a result of my reading them all on paper together. Granted, these were prayer requests that we all have.

But, reading them aloud felt as if prayer had been abridged to a honey-do-list for God.

You know, it really is okay to contact God just to chat sometimes. Does a request always have to be involved? It's perfectly fine to pray a request-less prayer of thanksgiving. And what if God has a few requests of us? Do we routinely ask? And then, do we wait long enough for Him to respond? (We'll talk about how to do that a little later).

Moreover, the vast majority of routine prayer requests are things that God already promised to do for us. He promised to supply all of our needs "according to His riches in glory" (Philippians 4:19). There is healing for us as well (Isaiah 53:5). Even the plan for prosperity has already been outlined for us in the scriptures (Joshua 1:7). Wouldn't it be grand if our faith level eventually elevated to a place where we no longer felt the need to clutter our prayers with the things our Heavenly Father knows we have need of and already promised to supply? Yes, we have a role to play by keeping His commandments. But, the point is, He already told us what to do to both obtain and maintain those things. Therefore, the greater portion of our prayer life should be focused on things such as how to love our enemies, getting our next assignment from God, being elevated to our next spiritual level, and any other spiritual needs more so than the temporal. Let us be reminded that God is a living being who has feelings, a personality, and a heart. If we could widen our visional scope, it could unveil a plethora of innovative prayer styles that would be refreshing to the ears of God.

When he was growing up, my eldest nephew Marquez was a talented, persistent kid who had taken a liking to my bride-to-be. Anytime she entered the room he would leap into her lap and guard her—kind of like my dog, Polo, does to me now. I don't know if it was his stubborn nature or if he found the vegetable unpalatable, but on one dinner occasion, my sister (his mother) was having a most difficult time convincing him to eat his broccoli. She even tried bribery to no avail. Being the youngest of the uncles, I rarely felt the need to assist with such situations. I would typically be in a corner somewhere chuckling at the drama. I got married at age nineteen, so as a teenager, this was hilarious to me. But my gal decided to pull from the bond she'd established with him and see if she could be more convincing. Where this thought came from, I'll never know. But, she decided to explain to him in grandiose terms that a piece of broccoli is actually a little tree. I wish you could have seen his eyes grow to the size of two shining quarters while his jaw dropped in amazement. "Little trees?" He uttered, seeking confirmation. "Yes. Little trees," she replied confidently. "Now, don't you want to eat a little tree?" What red-blooded boy wouldn't rise to such a challenge? We all watched quietly as he ate every piece of broccoli on his plate.

Well, that little boy grew up to become quite a healthy-looking specimen and is the tallest in our family. He'll eat virtually any home-cooked vegetable in sight. I recently reminisced on that broccoli-tree day as I watched him devour a plate complete with vegetables he'd fixed himself when he and his girlfriend dropped by my house last Thanksgiving. I wondered if that experience was a turning point for him. What if my wife hadn't stepped in? What if he grew up hating vegetables and had to take nutrition supplements for the rest of his life to survive? I wonder if that situation is what gave him the courage to go on to try cabbage, collards, and green peas.

I may never know the answers to those questions, but, *at that very moment, I learned a life-lesson*. *One situation can catapult you onto a completely different course of life and it matters not how or when or where that situation takes place. What matters is that you seize it when it happens.*

Prayer to a new Christian can be as foreign as broccoli was to my little nephew. The truth is, most of us Christians, if completely honest, view prayer as a necessary discipline that we don't have to enjoy; we just have to "do it" for the overall health of our spiritual lives or to get what we want from God. But what if there was an experience we could have that would cause us to change our mindset toward prayer?

Every Christian needs to have a broccoli/tree-eating experience regarding prayer. It's that moment when we realize what we are doing is much more than a discipline. Prayer enables us to believe we can accomplish the impossible. Through prayer, mountains become surmountable. Problems become solvable. Miracles become plausible. Prayer reduces the gigantic trees of life to little wilted pieces of broccoli that we can conquer one bite at a time. It's all in how you view life. And prayer is the spiritual binoculars we all need.

In my research, I stumbled across a list of kids' favorite vegetables. Broccoli was near the top. Green peas didn't even make the list. Why not? Well, kids rarely eat for nutritional value. They eat for taste. If it's not scrumptious, a kid will have a difficult time understanding why they should endure placing it in their mouth. It's the same concept that makes getting children to take medicine difficult. This is why they came up with all sorts of gimmicks to get kids to eat veggies and take medication. Whether it's a choo-choo train spoon slowly making its way inside a tunnel-like mouth or hiding finely minced broccoli inside of chocolate brownies, you have to do whatever will work. At the end of the day, if a child is malnourished, the parent is to blame. Try telling the Department of Human Services that the reason for your child's malnutrition is they didn't like vegetables and watch them cart your kid away in a moment, in the twinkling of an eye.

You are a *Christian*. You cannot expect to lead a successful Christian life if you don't eat the green peas of prayer. I don't want you to feel like you have to choke the peas down. I want you to enjoy them. What's so enjoyable about prayer? Don't forget that this is your opportunity to engage in conversation with The Lord God Almighty Jehovah-Jireh, himself! What a privilege and an honor that He would invite you to the conversation pit and let you talk with Him for as long as you desire. I now have high respect and value for the words to the hymn I learned at my Father's church as a young kid, "What a Friend We Have in Jesus." The verse goes on to say, "...what a privilege to carry everything to God in prayer." That privilege quickly manifests itself as a two-edged sword. For if we fail to take full advantage of this privilege, the hymnologist later tells of the peace we will forfeit and the needless pains we will bear. What a high cost to pay for merely bypassing a privilege. Therefore, I'd suggest that you reshape your view toward prayer into one that recognizes the honor that comes along with this privilege. Just as you would perhaps clear your schedule to accept an invitation to the White House, fail not to keep your established prayer times with God the Father. That's the true essence of the scripture, "Pray without ceasing" (1 Thessalonians 5:17).

Clearly you can't walk around speaking in tongues 24 hours a day. You'd get nothing accomplished and would likely get fired from your job. But you can endeavor to consistently meet God at a designated time regularly. God honors consistency.

I went through a period in my ministry when I felt led to rise early in the morning to have some prayer time with God. For whatever reason, the time of 4:30 a.m. dropped into my spirit. You would have to know me personally to understand the gravity of this sacrifice. That would be a cakewalk for my wife. But my daughter (mini-me) and I would rather chew rocks than get out of bed that early on any day for any reason—much less on a regular basis. It frightened me to embark on such a journey. It was as if I could hear Satan laughing in advance as he anticipated my defeat. Nevertheless, I set my alarm clock for 4:30 a.m. It took a few days for my body clock to accept the reality of the torment I was inflicting. The first few mornings, my sub conscience seemed to assume the alarm was for my wife but surely not for me. I recall dreaming that an alarm was going off and wishing someone would turn it off before I realized it was mine. I would look at the clock in amazement that it had been ringing for three or even five minutes before I realized I needed to turn it off. Let me just pause right here and say that snooze buttons are a tool of the enemy that work to enable the spirit of tardiness. Please, beware. I did a lot of repenting. But, the wonderful thing about God is that, if there first be in you a willing mind, it is acceptable (2 Corinthians 8:12). I love how God patiently waited for me to get myself together, morning after morning. I cannot tell you everything that happened for me during that timeframe, but I can tell you what didn't. I didn't morph into a morning person. And I no longer get up that early and pray. Personally, I still prefer studying and praying late at night. I feel more alert then, and I don't feel pressure from the clock to wrap it up because it's time to get ready for work. Night study feels limitless to me and God meets me there as well. He never sleeps or slumbers (Psalm 121:4). Here's what I did notice when making the sacrifice to rise early in the morning to pray: God consistently met me in some shape, form, or fashion. I was surprised by how quickly I felt His presence each morning. Now, I know that anytime I desire to commune, He is there as long as my setting is intimate, consistent, and sincere. Because God took me through that time of discipline, He now knows that if He needs me at 3 a.m., I'm available. I've proven myself.

Intercession is when you avail yourself to labor in prayer on behalf of someone other than yourself. While that may be easy to empathetically do when you understand the severity of the need, it can become more challenging as you grow in prayer and God presses upon you to pray for someone when you don't even know what's wrong.

One night I was awakened around 1 a.m. so forcefully that I thought it was a dream. The Holy Ghost clearly told me to get up and pray for one of our church members. I could sense that she was in some sort of trouble and the urgency was frightening. I got out of my bed and went into another room, so as not to wake my wife, and I began to pray. As I prayed, I could feel the enemy becoming angry that I was doing so, which, of course, prompted me to pray harder. Suddenly, I knew that she was being trapped by the enemy somehow, and I had to pray hard for God to have mercy because if He didn't, she was going to reap whatever she had sown. I still didn't have any details. I was praying out of spiritual obedience. But it's the effectual and fervent prayer of the righteous that avails, so I felt the need to turn it up a notch. I didn't know if God had other people praying for her or just me. However, I couldn't bear the thought of her losing this battle simply because I failed to have her back in prayer. So, I really began to beg God to have mercy. It was quite a struggle and went on far longer than I thought it would. I was exhausted by the time the Spirit released me back to bed. But, once my Spirit eased, somehow, I knew she had gotten the victory. This was on a Saturday night. When I got to church Sunday, tired from my late-night battle, a fleshy and bold Peter-like sprit came over me when I saw her. Before I knew it, I had marched right up to her and asked, "What on earth were you doing last night at 1:15 in the morning?" I wish you could have seen the look on her face. It was one of horror and shock with a hint of please-don't-make-me-answer-that-question. As her eyes welled up with tears, I said, "Never mind. I don't even want to know. But, let me tell you that God got me up out of my bed to pray for you and that might be the only reason you survived." And I think I mumbled something about her being somewhere she had no business being. Okay. So, I didn't handle that very well. But, that whole experience was a new one for me. I'm now appreciative that God would ever choose to use me in such a manner and have grown to know to use wisdom before calling someone out. If God uses you in such a manner, it may be wise to ask Him if He wants you to pray privately or notify the person for whom you're praying. Secret prayer has its purposes. Remember you're an instrument being used by God and for His glory, not your own.

God wants some of us to learn to **be persistent in prayer**. God is not a magician whom you ask to perform a trick. He divinely wills things into being based on our level of faith. But faith without works is "dead, being alone" (James 2:17-26). So, our prayers must be continual and mingled with faith. In the Bible, we find that Jesus shared a parable of a widow who asked a judge to avenge her of her adversary (Luke 18:1-8). The widow worried the judge so persistently that he decided he had better grant her the request because she was simply not going to leave him alone. Jesus goes on to ask, "How much more shall our Heavenly Father respond to the cries of His children?" The Old Testament prophet declared that, if we call God, He will answer, but when we cry, He will declare His presence (Isaiah 58:9). I don't want God to just give me an answer. I want Him to come and intimately be involved in the details of my situation. When we pray effectual and fervent prayers out of an honest heart, it helps a lot (James 5:16). Being righteous helps our prayers as well, but it's not enough. "Our righteousnesses are as filthy rags" (Isaiah 64:6) in God's sight because none of us will ever attain to His level of holiness. Therefore, because God is a spirit, it's not so much the words we use, but it's our level of intensity with which He identifies.

Previously, we skirted the notion that we should spend a portion of our prayer time waiting for God to speak to us. It sounds great when we announce that we're about to have a conversation with God. But, hearing His audible voice is not something we should routinely expect. I doubt we could barely stand it even if it did happen (Exodus 19:9-16). But there are ways that God speaks to us—even today. I want to give you some options regarding how you can hear from God and understand when He likely has spoken to you. God deals with each person differently. He may not deal with you in the same manner each time He speaks. But, as you grow spiritually, I promise, you will become familiar with how God speaks personally to you and the Holy Ghost will give you a feeling of peace and assurance that God has spoken. Here are a few guidelines:

Mental Clarity & Tranquility are important when it comes to setting the atmosphere in which God can and will speak to your heart. Because He is a spirit He must be perceived by humans for them to assure His presence. But, only a portion of man is spiritual. So, it helps to eliminate distractions and be focused so you can more easily tap into your inner spiritual realm. Turn the television off. Mute the cell phone. Get away from family, pets, and noise. Isolate yourself. Be quiet. Rid your mind of all distracting thoughts and concentrate on spiritual things. Typically, if the atmosphere is right, God will speak first. That strong thought that triggers a response from the Holy Spirit inside of you is often the voice or Spirit of God. When I say, "triggers a response from the Holy Spirit inside of you," I'm speaking of whatever your typical reactions are when God's Holy Spirit moves within you or touches your heart. That feeling of emotion manifests to bear witness to the fact that God has spoken. It's His spirit and they always have and always will work together. One of the main reasons that the Holy Spirit was given to man was to bear witness. So, expect the witness to manifest himself when God is speaking.

And he said, Go forth, and stand upon the mount
before the Lord. And, behold, the Lord passed by, and
a great and strong wind rent the mountains, and brake
in pieces the rocks before the Lord; but the Lord was
not in the wind: and after the wind an earthquake; but
the Lord was not in the earthquake:
And after the earthquake a fire; but the Lord was not
in the fire:
and after the fire a still small voice. And it was so,
when Elijah heard it, that he wrapped his face in his
mantle, and went out, and stood in the entering in
of the cave. And, behold, there came a voice unto
him, and said, What doest thou here, Elijah? (1 Kings
19:11-13)

Beloved, believe not every spirit, but try the spirits
whether they are of God (1 John 4:1)

Search the Scriptures during the times when you desire to hear
back from God. You don't even have to say amen and close your
prayer. After you've said all you have to say, earnestly ask God
to speak to you and grab a Bible. Search slowly and carefully as
you skim. When your eyes fall on the passage God wants you to
read, you'll feel that confirmation response from the Holy Spirit
as well. Sometimes you'll need to just start reading. There will
be times when you will be amazed at the precision. What you're
reading will often speak directly to your situation or answer your
question. There will also be times when what you're reading will
not seem applicable and you'll just need to continue reading or
turn to another passage. But, don't give up. Be patient. Remain
prayerful and do not try to hurry God. If it's not working out,
that could mean God wants to speak to you through some other
means and that's perfectly fine. It could also mean that God has
another course to which He is directing you to prepare you for
an upcoming situation wherein that particular Word will come in

handy. Time spent reading and meditating on the Word of God is always time well-spent and never wasted. Read in faith. Trust that God is in control. And always remember that the Word of God is in fact Jesus Christ (John 1:1-36). Jesus can speak too.

I was called by God into the ministry. This is a special time in one's life during which God is often teaching the called individual how to become familiar with His voice. I felt confident that God was calling me to do this work, but my flesh had some serious problems with me just stepping out in faith. What if I were mistaken? What if I were to make a fool of myself? What if I were to fail? Therefore, I wanted to be 100% sure. I remember spending a great deal of time asking God to make His will clear to me. However, He had already done that through various means. At this point, it was flesh gratification that I was seeking. Seeking faithless confirmation can anger God. But, sometimes He will appease us. That was the case with me. I told God I wanted him to show me through His Word that He wanted me to preach. After telling Him that, I picked up my Bible. As soon as I opened it, it fell on 1 Corinthians 9:16 which says, "...woe is unto me, if I preach not the gospel." Well, I didn't want to accept it, so I immediately flipped a chunk of pages to read something else hoping that was just a coincidence. I inadvertently flipped to Romans 10:15 which reads, "How beautiful are the feet of them that preach the gospel..." By now my heart was pounding. I decided to try this one more time. Sure enough, the next passage I flipped to was along the same lines. It was Luke 4:18: "The Spirit of the Lord is upon me, because he hath anointed me to preach the gospel..." I slammed the Bible closed and put it away and didn't pick it back up for quite some time. God had called my bluff. He knew I still wasn't ready to accept it. Yet, He left me with no excuse. By the time I accepted it, seemingly everyone in my circle knew I had been called. I'm glad God gave me the assurance I needed. Everybody who accepts a calling of this magnitude should be certain. It's that certainty that ensures success (2 Peter 1:10). But, you will still have to walk by faith. There's no getting around it. Failure to do so will result in God's displeasure regardless of how well you execute tasks (Hebrews 11:6). Familiarity with God's voice will help you in this area.

Because God used His Word to help me verify my calling, the Word has become a place of familiarity for me. Often I peruse the scriptures when I am seeking answers from God. It works for me. But, it's not the only method I'll use. Never try to force God's hand or box Him in to one method just because it's your preference. Be open. Remain attentive. Look for God to speak to you in multiple ways.

Gospel Music is a vehicle God uses. Many of the lyrics have been borrowed straight from the Holy Scriptures. Even if you don't get a direct answer from the words of a song, Gospel music is an effective tool you can use to set an atmosphere of spirituality. It can also help you clear your mind. Musicians, music, and singing each exist in heaven (Revelation 14:2-3). We should be grateful that God chose to reveal this heavenly art form to mankind early in his existence (Genesis 4:21), and it connects us to Him in more ways than we realize. I've found that even in times of temptation, I can sing a spiritual song and soon will realize that the enemy has been chased away and replaced by the presence of the power of God (Acts 16:25-26).

God uses sermons to speak to mankind. Any situation wherein the Word of God is being taught is often a means that God will use to speak. You could get your answer in Sunday Bible School, at a midweek Bible Study, a radio broadcast, tele-evangelism, social media, etc. There are so many ways that are now being used to spread the Gospel that we have no excuse. I've even been driving, looked up and saw a billboard message and immediately knew God was speaking directly to me.

Sometimes, **God uses others to prophetically speak** His will into our lives (1 Thessalonians 5:20). This is why it is so important to follow the Spirit of God when He leads. Have you ever had a long, lost friend who randomly is on your mind, and you can't stop thinking about him or her? It could be that God wants you to call and check on that individual or even pray for their well-being. I know I've had the phone ring and was surprised at who was on the other end. That person will go on to say something like, "God placed you on my mind, and I just want you to know that He heard your prayer and everything is going to be alright." What a faith-boost! And they tend to come just at the time when we are contemplating throwing in the towel. Maybe you should think twice before rejecting a call. An answer to prayer could be on the line.

SEVEN MORE REASONS WHY YOU SHOULD EAT THE GREEN PEAS OF PRAYER:

1. On average, you'll find six to seven green peas in a pea pod. Biblical numerology teaches that the number six is the number of mankind and the number seven denotes completion. No man's life is or ever will be complete without eating the green peas of prayer.

2. Green peas do not need heavy fertilizers. They don't even need a lot of water to grow. That's interesting because the seed pretty much has everything it needs to reproduce. Your prayer life doesn't have to be "extra." Just pray. Prayer will always do what it's designed to do. Just be sincere and have faith when you pray (Mark 11:24).

3. Much like the power of prayer, peas can take that which is dead and use it to spark new life. Did you know that you can add wood ashes to the soil and the pea roots will make use of it and thrive? So, pray about everything. Even pray about dead situations that seem hopeless. Prayer can bring

life to dead situations. Jesus performed a lot of miracles on the spot. But, when He got ready to raise Lazarus from his four-day old grave, Jesus spent some time in prayer to God first.

4. The oldest pea was found in Thailand, and it was over three thousand years old. However, green peas weren't discovered until the 18th century. It may take some time before you discover the greatness of the green peas of prayer. And I cannot tell you how long it might take. But I can tell you that unless you keep praying, you'll never make it to the greatness of that realm. So, keep praying. It's worth it.

5. In 1969 the first television commercial to be broadcasted in color was for Birds Eye Frozen Peas. After seeing these green peas in a brand-new way, television commercials changed forever. When God begins to transform you through prayer, people will see you like they have never seen you before, and if you continue fervently, you'll become changed forever.

6. Nine thousand peas are eaten per person per year in Britain. That's twenty-four peas per day, one for each hour. Therefore, you can keep a prayer going on in your heart every hour of the day.

7. Pea Green is regarded as a peaceful color that is well suited for the dining room that we might be at peace in the place where we eat. Feel free to use prayer to help make the atmosphere conducive for you to continue eating. There are more peas in the pages ahead.

Here are seven songs I recommend for your meditation and focus regarding prayer:

"The Lord's Prayer" by Psalmist Raine

"The Prayers" by J. Moss

"Pray" by CeCe Winans

"Every Prayer" by Israel Houghton/Mary Mary

"When We Pray" by Tauren Wells

"Prayed Up" by Karen Clark-Sheard

"The Altar" by Kirk Franklin

CHAPTER FIVE

Eat Your Promises (The Field Pea)

W e will use this chapter to expose you to the vastness of the promises of God. You will also come to understand why virtually everything Christians believe, achieve, and receive is a result of these promises. As we learn how God is the original promise keeper and will never come short of His Word, our faith becomes unwavering. This spiritual catch twenty-two effect propels the cycle that continuously unlocks even more promises as we grow. The possibilities are endless.

Field peas come in a lot of different varieties and as a title covers many peas like a blanket. One might even go as far as to say, "Can't all peas be grown in the field?" Absolutely. But this particular small reddish-brown pea never became widely known by any other name. So, we are going to call it the field pea, as it is currently and commonly known in the Deep South. They are readily recognizable, not only by their distinct size and color, but also their distinct and deceitfully strong flavor. The longer they cook, the more pot liquor is produced, and it is as deep red and brown as the pea itself, if not more so.

Although biblical promises come in a lot of different varieties, it's the word *promise* that covers Christians like a blanket. One could easily make the mistake of thinking a promise is a promise and one promise is as good as any, much like the assumption many make regarding the title of "field pea." But, I want you to learn the distinct flavor of each of God's promises. Don't walk through your spiritual life blindly with an attitude that is content to get whatever's coming to you. Be specific in your pursuit. Know exactly which promises you expect to benefit from and challenge yourself to measure up to the requirements expecting the fullness of each blessing to befall you. Promises might fall under the same umbrella, but each one of God's promises was created for a specific reason. And each of those reasons will support and stabilize you as you go on to reap each benefit.

Marriage is full of surprises and new experiences. Any time two lives come together, each brings its own set of traditions and values into the union. How the merger takes place is likely to determine the successfulness of the bonding process. You learn to stand up for the things that mean the most to you. You also learn not to sweat the small stuff. But, there's something interesting about traditions. They seem to mean a lot more to people than they perhaps should. Just because something has been done a certain way for a certain length of time doesn't mean your whole world is going to fall apart if it changes.

I was forced to begin learning this particular life-lesson early in my marriage. My wife is a Carolina girl who grew up in a small country town about thirty miles inland from Charleston. That region is known as the Low Country, and they march to the beat of their own drum. From the dialect to the food traditions, the South Carolina Low Country boasts of a rich heritage that is a unique conglomerate of Western Africa, the Caribbean Islands, and the Deep South. Remember, I was a sheltered kid from the country in Tennessee. If it didn't have a twang when spoken, I was likely to need it repeated before I understood. Suddenly I found myself thrust into a world full of Geechee talk and Gullah language. Sometimes it felt like I was visiting a foreign country. I was soaking it all up like a sponge and enjoyed learning until the holiday season rolled around and my world came crashing down. There I was in the kitchen on New Year's Day fixing my plate. Pot after pot of savory food covered the stove and each adjacent counter top. My plate was pretty much full except for the space I'd left for the black-eyed peas. When I got to the end of the counter and noticed that last pot didn't have the black-eyed peas in it, I realized I'd made some sort of mistake. How did I skip the black-eyed peas? So, I went back through the pots searching. My wife had that are-you-about-to-do-something-to-embarrass-me-in-front-of-my-family look on her face and being the outspoken belle that she is, she quickly asked, "What are you lookin' for?" I replied, "The black-eyed peas. Where are the black-eyed peas?" I'll never forget the way she looked at me. It was as if she wanted to ask me why but wasn't in a position to take the time. So, I got the blunt answer, "We don't eat black-eyed peas!" I didn't care if they ate them regularly or not. It was New Year's Day and *somebody* was gonna have to produce me at least one serving of black-eyed peas so as not to ruin my whole year. "Y'all don't eat black-eyed peas for New Year's?" I cried as a last-ditch effort in hopes that I'd misunderstood her previous declaration, although it was clear as a bell. "Naw! We eat Hoppin' John. Y'all don't eat Hoppin' John?" By now I'm feeling so many emotions, I can't even breathe. I know I'm deep in the Low Country, but I'm seriously thinking about running down to the nearest restaurant and finding me some black-eyed peas before sundown. I'm also angry because we didn't have this discussion earlier, or I would have cooked myself a pot. And I'm rather confused because I haven't the foggiest idea of who John is or why he hops, and I just want some black-eyed peas. I didn't know whether to call my Mama and cry or use this as a teachable moment for the entire Walker Family who obviously hasn't a clue as to what New Year's Day dinner is supposed to be. I've never been good at hiding my facial expressions. By now, my wife's grandmother is chiming in and asked me what was the matter. Before I could give a respectfully evasive answer, my outspoken better half tosses me right under the bus, "He lookin' for black-eyed peas! I told him we don't eat black-eyed peas. We eat Hoppin' John." And my grandmother-in-law began to laugh as she said, "You ain't neva had Hoppin' Johns?" but quickly curtailed her laughter once she realized how distraught I was. Like all grandmothers, and true to her nature, she handled the situation with love and grace. She pushed Nova out of the way, came near to me, picked up a spoon and began dipping into the pot as she said, "Here. Taste it. It's good. Ain't nuthin but some field peas and rice. And you like oxtails, ain't it?" "Yes, ma'am." I answered with a lump in my throat. Was I about to cry? Over some peas? What the heck is wrong with me? I told myself to man up and just deal with it. Truth is, I loved beef oxtails. I didn't realize that was an ingredient. And at least they did have the collard greens I was equally anticipating. I was still deeply disappointed because my tradition was broken. But, a new one did begin because Hoppin' John put black-eyed peas to shame. I must have eaten three helpings that day. Eventually, my wife's grandmother taught me how to make it, and whether in Carolina or Tennessee, I've not gone a year without Hoppin' John on New Year's Day since then.

As it turns out, black-eyed peas are one of those types of field peas I told you about earlier. They are all in the same family and come under the same umbrella. If you noticed the photo I included, you can see that the small red field pea also has a black eye in the center just like the black-eyed pea. So, when I ate the Hoppin' John dish, I was covered under my tradition and didn't even know it. I went through all of that drama and embarrassment for absolutely nothing. That's exactly how the promises of God work in our lives. The Bible outlines over two thousand promises. We'll never know them all. Neither will we ever fully understand how they work together on our behalf. But whether we realize it or not, as long as we stand on them, they've got us covered.

Don't think that these promises are for the saints alone. God has promises that are extended to sinners as well. Take the principle of tithing, for example. Money-handling expert and financial guru Dave Ramsey teaches that while it's fine to do so, businesses don't have to tithe out of their gross profits because there is not a biblical mandate instructing them as business owners to do so. He, as a tithing Christian, waits until the money comes home to him, and then he tithes on it as it is not true realized income until it comes home. Because he is the business owner, he feels that this is essentially like tithing the business. However, Nick. B. Nicholaou, President of Ministry Business Services, Inc. outlines tithing suggestions for business owners who want their business to be a tithing business. He teaches that businesses should tithe from their gross profits before any expenditures take place. He bases this principle on Leviticus 27:30-33 which instructs everyone to tithe from *everything* in the land because it all belongs to the Lord. This would include gross business profits, needless to say. I suppose you're wondering what I think. Well, I feel it depends on how you view your business. If the business is viewed as a separate entity and you merely control its operations, and you want it to be blessed in and of itself, tithe on it and pray for God to bless it accordingly. But if you view it as merely a source from which your income is derived as a business owner, you'd be tithing twice if you tithed it from its gross profits before expenditures and then tithed personally once you cut yourself a check. I do agree with Dave that there's nothing wrong with giving to God in this way. You're not going to be cursed for doing so. But, I've always felt in my heart that if I ever owned a business, I would want that business to tithe in and of itself. I think it serves as an example to the executives as well as the employees of the importance of intentionally supporting the up-building of God's kingdom in faith. As a result, we can expect God to bless our business efforts. What people do with their individual paychecks is their own business. But what I do as a proprietor over any finance-producing entity could cause me to be held accountable in the day of judgement and that's a risk I'd rather not take.

Tithing is a biblical principle that is attached to a promise. The internet is filled with stories of business owners who have adapted this principle to their businesses and attribute their success to having done so. Biblical promises are so certain that you can test them out to see if they work. Some may not even require faith. They just work. I remember teaching a Sunday Bible School class of young people, and the subject of tithing came up. One of the young men who had recently gotten a job was explaining to me how he couldn't afford to tithe because he always runs out of money before his next paycheck arrives. I explained to him that I couldn't afford not to tithe. But, I did challenge him to try God. I suggested to him that perhaps God is the one who has placed a hole in his pockets because He's tired of being robbed. He did agree to try paying his tithes at least once and see if God would stretch his money. The Sunday after doing so, he excitedly reported to the class that he couldn't explain how, but for the first time since he'd started working, he had money to bridge him until he got his next paycheck. He was so glad he paid his tithes. Moreover, *at that very moment, he learned a life-lesson. Tithing is a life-changing principle encased in the promises of God. If we are bold enough to try standing on His promises, He is bold enough to prove to us how true they are. Faith in action always has and always will move God.*

The promises of God are yea and Amen in Him (2 Corinthians 1:20). This means, to receive God's promise, the only thing we need is God, himself. We can put an "amen" on it and even that praise and glory is going back to Him. Essentially, everything is by God, from God, through God, and to God. I love the fact that God included His own "amen" in the Word. Everett Drake, one of our local Gospel music icons, wrote a song entitled, "Amen Goes Right There." Christians shouldn't have to be told when and where to put an "amen," but so often, we fail to do so. Sometimes, we even fail to recognize when and where "amen" should be. Don't wait for the promise to come to pass. Learn to praise God as a gesture to Him when you have decided to take Him at His Word. True believers in His Word already know, beyond the shadow of a doubt, that every word God has spoken will come to pass. Whether we are alive to witness it or not, we rest assured that it will transpire. This fact makes "amen" appropriate every step of the way. Moreover, if we choose not to utter "amen," The Word already has attached one to itself. How's that for a glimpse into the mindset of God? Stay connected to the hope of His promises. Eventually, you'll learn that they do come to pass.

I suppose it feels a little late to define the word promise, but I'm getting ready to do so. Not to insult your intelligence because I'm sure you already have some idea what the word means. However, words have more than one meaning. For the purposes of this book, I'd like for you to think about a promise as a binding declaration that gives the person to whom it is made a right to claim or expect the performance or forbearance of a specific act. That's thorough. Let's deal with forbearance for a moment. There are some things that God promised us He would *not* do. While it feels awesome to know that certain things won't befall us, these types of promises are often quite conditional. Such is the case with disease.

> And said, If thou wilt diligently hearken to the voice of the Lord thy God, and wilt do that which is right in his sight, and wilt give ear to his commandments, and keep all his statutes, I will put none of these diseases upon thee, which I have brought upon the Egyptians: for I am the Lord that healeth thee. (Exodus 15:26)

This promise was extended to God's children and was contingent on them hearkening diligently to God's voice as well as doing right per God's definition and listening to His commandments as well as keeping them. That's four major conditional areas. And for how long? A day of adherence? A month? A year? A decade? And what happens if I honor all four of these requests flawlessly for twenty years and then stop? Would it then be appropriate for me to contract a disease as a result of no longer keeping my end of the bargain?

We must also take into consideration what God meant when He identified himself as the God that healeth His people. Whenever you see *eth* at the end of a word, it means it is active right now and is ongoing continuously. I don't know where we got the notion that healing was something that was a one-time thing and then it's done. Nothing could be further from the truth. Just as our bodies are constantly aging and changing, healing is constantly taking place. Such is the case naturally. Our bodies are designed to heal themselves. All a surgeon can do is cut you open. He cannot put you back together again. He must sew or staple you together and hope that, if it holds your severed flesh together long enough, your body will form its own scab or keloid over time. When enough cells divide in all the right areas and for a long enough time, your body will heal itself. Surgeries will last a few hours, but your healing and recuperation period will last for weeks or even months. In some cases, your body will never be the same again. I love how God keeps man's knowledge limited. This is how He retains His position as the Supreme Being. While God is continually healing us through the amazingly complex bodily systems He created, there are some diseases that will not be fought off by your white blood cells. Our only hopes against a terminal disease are *divine healing* or *divine forbearance*; both of which are at the discretion of God. This is where the promise kicks in. I am not against being a health nut. It adds to your quality of life. But, healthy people contract terminal diseases every day. Healthy people also die every day. Then you have my mother who loved dark colas, hot sauce, Lay's potato chips, Starburst, and Hershey's almond chocolate bars but looked so young people frequently mistook her and my sister for siblings. Mom lived a holy life that paid off for her in many ways. She was a true beneficiary of many of God's promises. Life-claiming diseases are one thing, but sicknesses could be something different. While many illnesses are inherited, some do come as a result of us not taking good care of ourselves. Such sicknesses might be things that we've brought on ourselves as a result of the choices we've made versus the types of diseases God put on the Egyptians because they failed to acknowledge and obey Him.

Momma had her fair share of sickness. Some might even call it an unfair share. As her youngest child, I remember living in fear of growing up without a mother because she was hospitalized so frequently. I thought for sure that she was going to die before I made it to high school. It was nothing for Momma to be in the hospital for two or more weeks at a time. My sister, Theresa was eight years older and took amazing care of me during my elementary years whenever Momma was hospitalized. She cooked, cleaned, washed clothes, made sure I got my homework done, and nurtured me as if I were her son. My other sister, Belinda, who was six years older than me, while different from Theresa, filled a void as well. Although, she too was much older, she chose to condescend and play with me while Theresa managed things. My big brother, whom I looked up to, was the oldest of us all. He was twelve years older than me. So, by the time I was five, he was off in college and I missed him dearly. The lack of testosterone around the house was overwhelming at times, but the one person in my life who seemed to effortlessly balance everything out was Momma. But on this particular day, she wasn't there. I hated when she had to go into the hospital. Theresa was a great cook, but she wasn't Momma. And I suppose I could always ask my sisters to help me with my homework, but I knew they had their own school work to do. Momma would sit down and check my homework and lovingly help like only a mother could, but on this particular day, she wasn't there, and for whatever reason, it was going to hit me all at once.

It was Saturday. Daddy had gone up to the farm to work. Sometimes he would take me with him. Most of the time I enjoyed going with him; not so much because of the work, but it meant I got to spend some time with Dad, who wasn't home much due to his work schedule that frequently required him to travel. However, this time he didn't take me because I had chores and homework to do. At age seven or eight, there's not much to do when you finish your chores and homework. My sisters were teenagers with active social lives of their own. They never treated me like the plague. They took good care of me and often let me tag along, but I also knew at times they didn't want to be bothered with baby bro. This day, I wasn't sure exactly how the rest of my day was going to be spent. I was used to spending it with Momma while my sisters went about their routine, but she was in the hospital. I usually managed Momma's hospitalizations

in my mind better, but this was not a good day. Somehow, I felt
cheated in life. I felt tossed aside. I felt like life was treating me
unfairly. I wanted my Momma but there was nothing I could do
about it. So, I did what any option-less Momma's boy would do.
I burst into tears. I didn't plan to do it. It just hit me hard and all
at once, and I heard myself crying. Theresa was vacuuming with
a Kirby. If you've never heard a Kirby vacuum from the 1970's
you won't understand why I know it was an act of God that she
heard me crying and stopped vacuuming. She rushed over to me
and asked, "What's the matter?" I was too far gone to answer her
and didn't know what to say. I'd never cried like that before when
Momma was in the hospital, so saying that was the reason didn't
seem to justify the bitterness of my tears. But the same God who
sent her to me gave her discernment about my troubled, little
spirit. She calmly asked, "You miss Momma?" All I could do was
nod and continue my cry. I'll never forget how she grabbed me
that day. It wasn't a sister grab. It was a Momma grab. She held
me and said, "Don't cry. Momma's gonna be alright." She stayed
with me until I calmed down. I couldn't even go and visit her. At
that time, you had to be twelve years or older to be on certain
hospital floors. Daddy was a stickler for the rules, but my big
brother Victor would always sneak me in to see Momma. I would
stay with her until the mean nurses came and told me I had to
leave. But, Victor wasn't even there to sneak me in this time.
Could this day get any worse? I just wanted my Momma home. I
don't know if she realized it or if she meant to do it, but Theresa
made me a promise. She didn't use the words, 'I promise,' but a
promise it was, none the less. Did you catch it? She told me that
my mother was going to be alright. I believed her. Did she have
the power to make my mother get better? No, she did not. And
I knew she did not. But her words gave me hope. And hope is
the bridge to faith. And we were a God-fearing, Bible-believing,
faith-filled family. Therefore, if she had faith enough to tell me
that my mother was going to be alright, that was good enough for

me. Needless to say, God did eventually touch my mother's body and bring her safely home.

Theresa used one sentence to bridge her baby brother from hopelessness to faith that day. Sometimes, it's necessary for you, as a Christian, to bridge afflicted and oppressed people from their downtrodden depressed places to a place of faith. That can be done by declaring a promise of God. Theresa couldn't heal Momma, but we all had faith that God would. It's the fact that we stand on His promises that causes us to experience triumph in everyday life. If we believe it, we should declare it.

> Declare his glory among the heathen, his wonders
> among all people.
> For the Lord is great, and greatly to be praised: he is
> to be feared above all gods.
> For all the gods of the nations are idols: but
> the Lord made the heavens.
> Honour and majesty are before him: strength and
> beauty are in his sanctuary.
> Give unto the Lord, O ye kindreds of the people, give
> unto the Lord glory and strength.
> Give unto the Lord the glory due unto his name: bring
> an offering, and come into his courts.
> O worship the Lord in the beauty of holiness: fear
> before him, all the earth.
> Say among the heathen that the Lord reigneth. (Psalm
> 96:3-10)

There are also times during which God bestows supernatural healing through faith, on the spot. Some people do not believe in this power, but I have experienced it many times. I've experienced it in my own body, and I've experienced it while laying hands on and praying for others. Instant healing occurs when all of the biblical conditions, including faith, are aligned with the divine will of God.

I was having excruciating neck pains that progressively grew worse, and eventually I had to consult a physician. He took an x-ray of my neck and pointed out to me how the bones in my neck had basically grown crooked. He stated that there was nothing he could do to correct this problem. He suggested that I see a chiropractor, and I would have to do so for the rest of my life for temporary relief. So, I sought out the best chiropractor in the city to whom many of the Tennessee Titans NFL players went. He was great. And when I left there, I felt great. But, within two weeks I could feel my neck slowly tightening, and soon, I would need to return for another treatment. After nearly a year, I grew weary of this routine. However, I never specifically asked God to heal me, although I strongly desired such. I remember the last time I was lying on that long, flat table waiting for the chiropractor to come in and saying to the Lord that I didn't want to live like this. I wasn't requesting to be taken out of this world. I was letting Him know that I was tired of being in my current condition. It is so true that God will give His children the desires of their heart. God knew I wanted to be healed.

One Wednesday night after my neck had retightened, we were in a Bible study and the Spirit of God came mightily in the room near the end. The pastor stated that there was healing in the room and encouraged everyone to stand up and worship the Lord. I can honestly say that I never thought about myself. I stood out of obedience and found myself quickly catapulted in the spirit and was enjoying my worship experience for quite some time. Later, after we all had taken our seats, I haphazardly turned my head to one side for some reason. I'd become so accustomed to the pain that I knew to brace myself whenever I had to turn, and in most cases I would avoid doing so. This time when I turned, I felt no pain. I was shocked. I then began turning my head in every direction possible to make sure I wasn't mistaken. There was absolutely no pain. Although slightly out of order, I sprang to my feet and requested to testify. I didn't want to waste a moment declaring that God had healed my body. I couldn't afford to wait and risk giving an opportunity for doubt to creep in and cancel out my healing. I have not been to a chiropractor since, and my neck is perfectly fine. That was many years ago.

I've also seen God deliver my daughter from nutritional rickets. She was thirteen months old and still not walking. The doctors said they didn't know if my daughter would ever walk. They prescribed a medication that was seventy-five dollars per bottle. When my wife and I were discussing if we should continue buying this medication or trust God, my daughter accidentally knocked it and the bottle hit the floor and broke into probably a hundred pieces. All of that money went to waste. We immediately agreed to trust God. Not only is my daughter walking, but she is also an international cheerleading champion with more medals than I care to count.

There was also the time when my wife came home from the doctor with a report that her bloodwork was consistent with that of systemic lupus. That was over twenty years ago. My wife does not have lupus. I rebuked that report in the name of Jesus and believed God for her healing from whatever weapon was trying to form. Her bloodwork is consistently normal.

Because these things are promised in the Word of God, the only thing standing between you and your healing is your level of understanding regarding the conditional promises of God. I dare you to believe God and stand on His Word. When you meet the requirements, you can both command and expect your healing when it is aligned with His divine will.

We've discussed tithing which is an example of an automatic promise. We've also discussed healing which is a conditional promise. Finally, we need to discuss promises that are specifically tied to our faith. Faith unlocks so many things in our lives. But, I dare say that we cheat ourselves out of more promises through faithlessness than anything else. "Heal the sick, cleanse the lepers, raise the dead, cast out devils: freely ye have received, freely give" (Matthew 10:8).

Jesus gave His disciples power to do a lot of things. And once we receive the Holy Ghost, we have the ability to operate at that same level of power. Believe it or not, this passage is a promise extended to believers. This is quite an impressive list, isn't it? Of the above list, did any particular phrase cause you to second guess your personal ability to do so through the Holy Ghost? Did "raise the dead" stick out to you? Do you believe you have the power to raise the dead? Most Christians don't believe they do. And if you are among them, don't feel badly. Most preachers don't believe they do either. Okay, maybe both should feel badly. But whether you believe you have the power or not, it's a promise in the Word of God. It just requires a special type of faith to unlock it.

Death is certain. Being raised from the dead is not. So perhaps the wide-spread doubt among Christians is encased in the fact that we know at some point we are going to die anyways, so we feel we can't stop the inevitable. It also could be that we believe whenever God decides He wants us to raise someone from the dead, He will tell us to do so, and until then, we'll leave the dead, dead. I hope it's not that you think this is some figurative meaning and Jesus was talking about people who were spiritually dead and not physically dead. I'm sorry to disappoint you, but everything theologically and historically surrounding this text suggests that Jesus meant exactly what He said. I'm sure you know that Jesus raised the dead on many occasions (Luke 7; Luke 8; John 11). But aside from Jesus, prophets of old and New Testament apostles raised the dead. Elijah, Elisha, Paul, and Peter were each accredited as having done so (1 Kings 17; 2 Kings 4; Acts 9; Acts 20).

Death is certain. However, that has not always been the case. When God first created man, he was not to die. He was to live forever in the paradise of the Garden of Eden. Not until the sin of disobedience was man banished and eventually did "surely die" as was promised per the Word of God, Himself (Genesis 3:1-24).

I also just told you that being raised from the dead is not certain. However, after the trumpet sounds, the dead in Christ are going to rise first (1 Thessalonians 4:16). But, then there is going to be a second resurrection during which all others who are dead will stand before God and be judged (Revelation 20:6, 12).

If all of these things are true spiritually, then there is no reason why we, as believers, cannot raise the dead or shouldn't be able to do so. God sits in eternity. Death is a reality for us, but for Him it is as futile a factor as is sickness, sin, and sleep. But unlocking this promise requires faith in God's ability as well as confidence in the power of one's own prayer as they align with the Spirit-revealed divine will of the same God. If these elements come together, the dead both can and will be raised.

Late one Saturday evening, my sister Belinda had a vision wherein she saw herself lying dead in a casket. I was there when she began screaming while seeing this vision. Belinda was a teen-age minister who often had spiritual experiences, but this one seemed to outweigh them all. She didn't explain all of this to her terrified little brother, but the Holy Spirit had explained to her that God needed to take her on out of this world so that others would believe and give their lives to Him. She didn't fully understand, but she was willing to go. The next day, she was slated to bring the Word of God. She preached like never before. She seemed to be illuminated while she powerfully spoke. I can still see her in my mind as she ended her message with a smile, placed her Bible under one arm and waved to the congregation with her free hand while bidding them farewell. She exited the pulpit and collapsed. After that, everything was so chaotic, the details were blurry. But I do remember that I deemed this situation as another one that demanded my tears. I didn't want my big sister to die. But, there she lay on the floor unresponsive. I remember how pale her skin looked. My mother said her flesh was cold. So many people were gathered around, and they were all praying and crying out to God. My mother was spanking her cheeks trying to get a reaction, but there was none. Someone called the paramedics in faith that they would be able to revive her somehow. Maybe she had just fainted. I remember the paramedics telling us to get out of the way. Some did move, but most stayed close and continued praying and begging God to raise her up. Then, the worst possible thing that could have happened did happen. One of the paramedics said he couldn't get a pulse. After doing a few other things, he pronounced her dead. I heard him myself. I was mortified. But, I noticed that the saints simply kept praying as if the paramedic was a figment of their imagination. That paramedic stood straight up, wagged his head and proceeded to snicker at the praying saints as if to mock their tenacity. Again, he told us, a little louder this time, that she was dead. My mother kept calling my sister's name. The paramedic was packing his things to leave. I think he mumbled something about calling the coroner. But, the church never gave up and never stopped praying.

As my sister tells the story, she says that when she exited the pulpit, she saw another vision of a long stairway. It was as she started walking up that stairway that she collapsed. She said she could feel her body numbing. It started at her feet and proceeded up her body until her spirit left her. For whatever reason, God responded to the relentless prayers of the saints that day. Eventually, my sister opened her eyes. The paramedic was stunned. His facial expression was one of shame and medical astonishment. I'd like to think I had a hand in raising the dead that day as I was begging God right along with my mother and the rest of the congregants. But whether I did or didn't, one thing is for sure: That experience stratospherically catapulted my faith. At that point, I didn't know that God would eventually call me into the ministry, as He already had done for each of my siblings. But, it's hard to lead people spiritually when your faith is low. Since that day, God has used me to heal cancer, open blinded eyes, and cast out demons. And while I do have great faith, I must admit, it blows my mind every time God steps in and works the miracle. You see, I'm not what you would call a miracle worker. I neither have the gift of healing nor am an exorcist. But, I am a believer who has full faith in the fact that every promise God extended to us according to Matthew 10:8 includes me. I may not be able to empty a hospital, and I may not be able to put a mortician out of business. However, the level of faith I have, while it needs to be improved, is currently strong enough for me to consistently pray and ask God to do impossible things, and every now and then, He does them.

Someone once argued the point that Jesus told his disciples to do these things. So, why are we asking God to do them? If we already have the power, we should just obey His Word and do them. Well, this is where the beauty of our relationship with God as servants to Him shines brightly. A true servant *never* desires to do anything that is out of the will of his master. Sometimes, it is God's will that an individual dies. Sometimes, a Christian's faith is being tested, and we need not intervene. I've found that there are times when God imparts His will to me, and there are times when He does not. However, I must operate in faith that whenever a prayer request does not come to pass, it might not have been in the will of God; and that's okay with me. It doesn't bruise my ego. Now, there are times when my faith is higher than others. We also know, according to Jesus' teaching, that some promises are unlocked for certain situations through prayer and fasting—both of which serve to increase our faith. The goal is to not let the fault be in us as it often is.

Unlocking promises can be hard work. Be encouraged to do all you can to stand on these promises that God has given us. The harder you try to do so, the more you'll grow. And the more you grow, the further your faith will go. The further your faith goes, the more promises God will open for you. The only limitations are the ones set by you.

SEVEN MORE REASONS WHY YOU SHOULD EAT THE FIELD PEAS OF PROMISES:

1. For generations, field peas were grown in the rice and corn fields just for the nutrients they added back into the soil. Their sole purpose was to help the other vegetables grow. Every promise God made was designed to help His children in some way. But unless you plant your hopes and dreams in God's field of promises, you'll never realize the fullness He has reserved for you.

2. Field peas are known for being able to thrive in adverse conditions. Whenever you stand on God's promises, they work regardless of what adversities the enemy may throw your way. Satanic plots are always powerless against God's promises.

3. There was a time when field peas were considered the food for those who were in poverty. Who else is more flawlessly positioned to benefit from God's promises than the poor? Jesus promised the Kingdom of Heaven to the poor in spirit. Those who are less fortunate are poised to believe because they have a need. Never become so prosperous that you fail to see the need to lean on God's promises. The benefits are more than meets the eye.

4. One reason field peas were eaten by the poor is because they were so plentiful. Today, hundreds of heirloom varieties exist. Had they been a rare commodity, they would have likely been hoarded and given great value. There are so many promises in God's Word that theologians can't agree on exactly how many there are. Don't make the mistake of failing to value these promises. You'll be cheating yourself out of blessings if you do.

5. Field peas were brought over to America with the Africans when they were transitioned as slaves. Regardless of what transitions you go through in life, be sure to hand the promises of God down from your generation to the next. Teach your children to take them everywhere they travel in life.

6. Jeff and John Coykendall have spent years working in the area of field pea search and rescue. This means, they search the country looking for obscure varieties of peas. Let me encourage you to search the scriptures (John 5:39). With so many promises, you're sure to be busy for quite some time. And, if you search diligently, you're sure to find an obscure treasure God has promised to you that can change your life forever.

7. Last, but perhaps most important, field peas are the least expensive of peas. God's promises will not cost you any money. But what little you provide in exchange will be of no comparison to the bountiful blessings that will flow your way.

Here are seven songs I recommend for your meditation and focus regarding promises:

"Promise Keeper" by Fred Hammond & RFC

"Standing on the Promises" by Daryl Coley

"The Promise" by The Martins

"Standing on the Promises of God" by Alan Jackson

"The Promise" by Tiff Joy

"Promises" by Desperation Band

"For I Have Heard Your Cry" Marvin L. Winans Presents: The Praise & Worship Experience

CHAPTER SIX

Eat Your Persecution
(The Snow Pea)

ersecution is a plateau unlike any other. So, expect to be elevated to a new spiritual level after reading this chapter. You will become enlightened about the manner in which modern-day American Christians have suffered (and will continue to suffer) for the cause of Christ. Additionally, you'll be thoroughly educated on the mindset you must maintain throughout this necessary consequence of Christianity. Finally, you'll learn to and from where you should draw the strength you'll need to endure.

I'm sure you immediately noticed that the snow pea looks different from any of the other peas we've studied thus far. Some might even argue that it's not a pea at all. But, if you look closely at the above picture, you'll notice that there are tiny peas bulging from within each pea pod. These particular peas come with their own unique covering. You might consider it a package deal. And, if the truth be told, when you eat snow peas, you barely notice the inner peas. Taste wise, it's all about the package.

Such is the case with what I'm going to call the art of persecution. Whenever a mature Christian is enduring persecution, he recognizes when he is being persecuted. However, the actual bulges of persecution are concealed by that which covers him. This all-powerful and ever-concealing cover manifests itself in one of three forms: Faith, the Holy Ghost, and/or the Word of God. The covering serves a dual purpose. It protects the Christian by minimizing the impact. It also creates a mask on which the world can focus as they observe your persecution period and anxiously await the outcome. Later, in this chapter, we'll explore each of the previously-mentioned covers.

The word *persecute* is most simplistically defined as ill-treatment of an individual. However, it is most appropriately considered persecution when the ill-treatment happens as a result of a person's race, political beliefs, or religious profession. While the term *ill-treatment* seems to suggest something that is mild and tolerable, synonyms for *persecution* include words like tyrannize, abuse, torture, and even martyr. The word persecution comes from the Latin word *perscut* which means "followed with hostility." I suppose I'd braced myself for the word *hostility* but *followed* is the word that pours salt into the wound. It suggests that people will not only dislike and mistreat you, but they will also pursue you in an effort to perpetually inflict harm. If you are striving to live a Christian lifestyle, you are sure to suffer some form of persecution before you leave this world. "Yea, and all that will live godly in Christ Jesus shall suffer persecution" (2 Timothy 3:12).

I know you're probably thinking, "Perhaps over in the Middle East where the Bible has many of its origins, people will suffer persecution but surely not in the United States of America. We have laws in place to protect us from such treatment." Yes we do. But, we also have laws in place to keep us from jaywalking, speeding, drunk driving, and recreational drugs. Yet, each of those things take place on a daily basis and, unfortunately, goes unchecked more often than not. Such lawlessness has increased over time and is evolving just as Jesus taught his disciples that it would. Furthermore, we have a heinous history that includes civil war, terrorism of the Indians who were already rightfully here when Mayflower landed, and we need not even mention the cruelty of slavery. So, it's not farfetched to entertain the possibility of a reversion back to some form of such things especially given the current societal trends and widening division within our melting pot.

> Then shall they deliver you up to be afflicted, and shall kill you: and ye shall be hated of all nations for my name's sake. And then shall many be offended, and shall betray one another, and shall hate one another. And many false prophets shall rise, and shall deceive many. And because iniquity shall abound, the love of many shall wax cold. (Matthew 24:9-12)

I realize this information is disheartening. It might even cause some to reevaluate their desire to be a Christian in the first place. Suffering is suffering, and I dare not sugarcoat it. But I will say that if you are filled with the Baptism of the Holy Ghost, you will learn that the Spirit of God has a way of ushering the saints of God through adversity just as the snow pea's pod is ever standing by, ushering its inner peas.

> And I will pray the Father, and he shall give you an-
> other Comforter, that he may abide with you for ever;
> even the Spirit of truth; whom the world cannot re-
> ceive, because it seeth him not, neither knoweth him:
> but ye know him; for he dwelleth with you, and shall
> be in you. I will not leave you comfortless: I will come
> to you.... Peace I leave with you, my peace I give unto
> you: not as the world giveth, give I unto you. Let not
> your heart be troubled, neither let it be afraid. (John
> 14:16-18, 27)

I realize how blessed I am to be living in the United States of America where I am free to worship God. Therefore, I do not know what it's like for people in other countries who are physically persecuted for professing faith in Jesus. My heart goes out to missionaries and evangelists across the globe who risk their lives to spread this Gospel and often suffer accordingly. To whom much is given, much is required. Sometimes, I think it's because we have it so good that we can't even stand to endure a little name-calling. Yet verbal and mental abuses are both styled as forms of persecution. I call it mild persecution because our lives are not threatened. However, I do believe that we are living in a time when Satan is using this form of persecution as an effort to subtly destroy the influence of the body of Christ. It has become important in society to be socially accepted. So much so that young people are committing suicide as a result of being bullied or socially outcasted. Teenagers have been prescribed medication because they are depressed over degrading comments that have been made about them via social media. Defamation of character has been the basis of many lawsuits. In this type of society, how can a modern-day Christian see the need to endure verbal persecution for the cause of Christ?

I've never been physically persecuted. But I would like to share with you my testimony of how God conditioned me to endure mild persecution. Just prior to the year 2000, I found myself jobless again. I went through a temporary agency which finally sent me to work at a stock brokerage firm because it was available. However, my laid-back business office background seemed to be in direct contrast to the nature of this job. If you've ever seen the bustling environment of the New York Stock Exchange on television, you'll be able to understand exactly what I'd gotten myself into. People routinely shouted codes mingled with profanity back and forth in a chaotic atmosphere. I was a quiet, mild-mannered church boy, and all of this chaos made me nervous and uncomfortable. This was no environment for a Christian. Furthermore, the unscrupulous things people did to make money were a lifestyle I had no desire to live. Not to mention the fact that math was my worst subject. Why would God thrust me into the financial institution?

To my surprise, a few weeks into my three-month temp contract, my boss offered to buy me out of the contract if I would accept their offer of a full-time position with full benefits. I was shocked. I felt my performance was mediocre at best. I wasn't loud and worldly like the majority of that crew. I didn't fit in at all. I never accompanied them to the bar to unwind and drink at the end of the day. I never cussed or threw chairs across the room as was their custom to express anger or relieve stress. I even insulted a broker who tried to give me an expensive bottle of wine for Christmas by giving it back to him because I didn't drink. Everyone looked at me as an oddball. I thought I should turn him down and just work out my contract and keep looking for a better job to suit my demeanor. But, the Lord let me know in no uncertain terms that He had blessed me with that job, and I was there for a reason. So, I accepted.

It wasn't long before the mild persecution started. The lady who was to train me hated my guts for no apparent reason. No matter how smiley and sweet I was, she seemed to wax worse. She sighed and snapped so often that I asked her if I had done something to offend her, and she just ignored my question as if I didn't matter at all. That same day, God allowed me to see that an evil spirit was controlling her. I came to work early one morning and sat in her chair and prayed long and hard. I anointed everything on her desk that I could get my hands on with holy blessed oil and rebuked every spirit that was not like God. For three days she didn't say a word to me. On day four her attitude drastically improved. By the end of the year, she was laughing with me and even bought me a Christmas gift. *I learned a life-lesson in that very moment. When Jesus taught that we must love our enemies, He was serious. God can give you the ability to demonstrate love for an individual's spiritual well-being when your attempts at friendship have failed. But once agape love is put into action, it can conquer everything else.*

A new temporary employee surfaced. His personality was far more boisterous than mine and unlike me he seemed to fit right in with the brokers on the trading desk. He was a nice guy, and I'd hoped I'd finally found a potential friend as he introduced himself to me, and we became cordial. But once I learned how little we had in common, I doubted if our cordiality had much chance of blossoming into a friendship. I soon became jealous of how well he had fit in with them. They didn't need any friends and I was hoping God had sent one for me. I lost that hope rather quickly.

I never hid the fact that I went to church often, was quite active within my church, and that I was a minister of the Gospel. My new colleague thought it was strange for a man as young as me to dedicate so much time there. So, on Monday mornings, he had no qualms about loudly asking me, "How was church, Sunday?"

because he knew that's where I'd been. I gleefully told him what a great time we had while he gave me that same look you give people when you ask them how they are doing and they give details that you never wanted to hear in the first place because you were merely being cordial.

One Friday, I had no idea that ill-treatment was about to commence. This new colleague went around the room loudly asking everyone what they were doing that night. Everyone shared their answers proudly. He intentionally saved me for last and said, "Hey, William! Whatchoo doin' tonight?" Before I could respond, he yelled, "Oh that's right! You gon' be at CHURCH TONIGHT!" And he roared in laughter. Needless to say everyone joined in. I didn't know whether to be mad or embarrassed or if I should just laugh it off with everyone else. Well, typically, I can take a good joke when it's all in good fun. The problem was I didn't find this humorous at all. I suppose it would have been fine had it been a one-time thing, but this became his joyful ritual every Friday afternoon like clockwork.

You must remember, I belong to a small Pentecostal-Holiness church, and we believe in making God the priority rather than squeezing him into our schedules. Unlike a lot of other church organizations, we were engaged in worship three days out of the week. Most people he knew went to church once per week and possibly mid-week Bible Study. The fact that I was in my twenties and did so more than that qualified me as a religious fanatic in his eyes, and he felt the need to make a spectacle out of me. I was accustomed to being an outcast. I was not accustomed to public humiliation, embarrassment, and degradation. All I wanted was to find a way to fit in, and he had permanently dashed my hopes of such. Thanks to this new guy, I was the laughingstock of the stock brokerage firm. And it wasn't long before I dreaded going to work and grew weary of trying to circumvent these attacks and plastering smiles on my face to hide my disgrace.

Finally, the Friday came when things were about to change. He started his typical rant, and as I was bracing myself for the punchline, I heard the Spirit tell me to invite him to church. I thought, "Well, thanks a lot, God. I guess you want me to be a glutton for punishment. You know good and well this dude is *not* church material; much less, *Holiness* church material. And you know he's gonna decline my invite. But, fine, I'll invite him." Following my mental conversation with God, I heard this colleague give his usual, "I guess you're going to church tonight!" followed by laughter with the rest of the crew. But this time I chimed in just as loud as he was laughing and proudly replied with a smile, "That's right! I'm going to church, and you ought to come too, sometime!" "Well, maybe I will!" he sarcastically responded. One of the brokers said, "William, I cannot go to church with you or anyone else. I'm afraid as soon as I walk in the door, I'll burst into flames!" It was a welcomed diversion from the tenseness of the transition I'd introduced. And this became my regular response each Friday. I think he personally found the pushback refreshing. Although I was a bit of a stick-in-the-mud, he learned that I was cooler than he'd originally thought. He didn't accept my invitation, but it bridged us to developing a nice rapport amid the periodic, mild persecution that continued for over a year.

Shortly after my daughter was born, God clearly told me to start a songwriting career. I entered an international songwriting contest and was selected as a finalist. However, the finals were being held in Estes Park, Colorado, and I didn't have enough money to fly out there. This same harassing co-worker told me that he felt like I'd better not pass up this opportunity and volunteered to drive me if I wanted to rent a car and go. I found myself in a vehicle driving twenty hours across the country with a sinner whom I barely knew. But God had strategically orchestrated that trip. We became the closest of friends. I kept pitching gospel music CDs until I found one that he enjoyed, and it happened to be

Fred Hammond. So, we listened to Fred Hammond for nearly twenty hours between discussions. Once we got to Colorado, he said that was the longest he'd ever gone without a cigarette or drinking since he'd started some years back. He told me that he didn't know people could have so much fun without smoking and drinking, and he was really having a good time. Well, a blind man could have seen that spiritual door swinging wide open. So, I ministered to him for the rest of that trip. I thought surely I was going to win this soul. We got back home, and he still wouldn't come to church with me. But the seed had been firmly planted. I'd done my part. And I never stopped inviting him.

Finally, he did come to church with me. Ironically, it was on a Friday night. Our bishop was in town during our state convention to which I'd invited him. This consecrated annual assembly always carried a powerful anointing, and I'd begun praying for God to save my new friend. The Word of God went forth, and the Holy Ghost began to fall. He became convicted and found himself at the altar calling on the name of Jesus. We were all gathered around, praying with him and worshipping and singing until God miraculously saved his soul. To see him dance under the power of God and speak in tongues as he shouted and praised made every day on the job worth it. Not only did God deliver him from profanity, drugs, intoxication, and cigarette smoking, but, He called him into the ministry, blessed him with a Holy Ghost-filled wife, and he now assists me in the ministry at the church I pastor.

Neither of us worked for that company for a long time. I later learned that he had no financial background or experience that would qualify him to work in that industry either. He too was shocked when they offered him a job. Now that I look back on that situation, God brought us together because He needed to introduce this man to Jesus. Who knew he was one of God's anointed? And the persecution was designed by Satan to deter me from the task at hand. What if I'd quit the job? What if I'd exercised my right and turned him in to the HR department? What if I'd lost my temper and cussed him out to save face? I was certainly tempted to. What if I'd never accepted the job in the first place because I didn't feel that I was well suited for it?

I shared this story because I know many of you have been in similar situations. It's so easy to become selfish and make hasty decisions out of frustration without consulting The Lord. Doing so could cause you to hoist yourself right outside of the will of God. Stay calm. Pray. Trust God. Know that He's at work. Be patient. Endure hardness as a good soldier (2 Timothy 2:3).

From that situation, I learned that persecution should be dissected. God does not allow His children to suffer persecution for naught. If He allows it, there is a purpose. Therefore, if we operate in wisdom and faith, we'll consult God for advice on how we should respond and patiently wait for the manifestation of the victory the Word has promised us.

> For I reckon that the sufferings of this present time are not worthy to be compared with the glory which shall be revealed in us. (Romans 8:18)

> Many are the afflictions of the righteous: but the Lord delivereth him out of them all. (Psalm 34:19)

I also learned that we should welcome persecution, not because we enjoy pain, but because of the spiritual benefits we anticipate from having suffered for the cause of Christ and for the sake of His Gospel. It may take a while. But if God's Word is true, and we know it's true, benefits are sure to eventually manifest.

> Blessed are ye, when men shall revile you, and persecute you, and shall say all manner of evil against you falsely, for my sake. Rejoice, and be exceeding glad:

for great is your reward in heaven: for so persecuted they the prophets which were before you. (Matthew 5:11-12)

And whether we be afflicted, it is for your consolation and salvation, which is effectual in the enduring of the same sufferings which we also suffer: or whether we be comforted, it is for your consolation and salvation. And our hope of you is steadfast, knowing, that as ye are partakers of the sufferings, so shall ye be also of the consolation. (2 Corinthians 1:6-7)

Beloved, think it not strange concerning the fiery trial which is to try you, as though some strange thing happened unto you: But rejoice, inasmuch as ye are partakers of Christ's sufferings; that, when his glory shall be revealed, ye may be glad also with exceeding joy. If ye be reproached for the name of Christ, happy are ye; for the spirit of glory and of God resteth upon you: on their part he is evil spoken of, but on your part he is glorified. (1 Peter 4:12-14)

I didn't pass that test with an A+, but I passed. I didn't suffer in the best manner, but I endured. I wanted to give up on converting this dude, but I kept praying for him. The spirit is willing, but the flesh is weak. Keep your sprit strong, so you will be poised to follow it, regardless of how loud your flesh is screaming.

Let's talk about what covered me during that period of persecution. Previously, we mentioned three coverings. Your covering may change as you go through prolonged persecution. Initially, I hadn't a clue that God was at work, so it wasn't faith that covered me. Neither did I realize that the circumstance was a spiritual matter, so I wasn't quoting the Word of God. I just felt teased or bullied, and the topic just happened to be churchy. So early on, I believe it was the Holy Ghost who was my covering.

God only permitted the Holy Ghost to share bits and pieces with me about the situation as it was developing. This is a form of teaching that often takes place in the school of experience. This caused me to dually learn quite a few things about myself along the way and should have helped me not repeat the same mistakes next time. While the Holy Ghost knew He couldn't tell me everything, He did give me instructions, and I did obey them. He helped me hold my peace. He helped me keep my job. He helped me tolerate a personality that was unlike mine. He helped me learn how to thrive in an environment that was unlike any I'd had to be in before. How can we be effective leaders in the body of Christ, if we can barely stand being around people who have not yet become Christians? They don't look or act like us, but they need us, and we can't turn up our noses at them. We'll never be able to gain them.

> And as he passed by, he saw Levi the son of Alphaeus sitting at the receipt of custom, and said unto him, Follow me. And he arose and followed him. And it came to pass, that, as Jesus sat at meat in his house, many publicans and sinners sat also together with Jesus and his disciples: for there were many, and they followed him. And when the scribes and Pharisees saw him eat with publicans and sinners, they said unto his disciples, How is it that he eateth and drinketh with publicans and sinners? When Jesus heard it, he saith unto them, They that are whole have no need of the physician, but they that are sick: I came not to call the righteous, but sinners to repentance. (Mark 2:14-17)

If you don't have The Holy Ghost/Holy Spirit let me encourage you to receive Him as soon as possible. He is not an *it*. The Holy Ghost is an intelligent being and most viable constituent of the Godhead. He is God manifested in the form of a Spirit who is able to take up residence within our human bodies. He acts as a liaison between God the Father and us. We receive Him through the power that God gave to the name of His Son and that name is Jesus. So, they all work together as one and are one. People argue that the Trinity is not a biblical principle and should not be taught. While it's a fact that the word Trinity does not exist in the Bible, the doctrine of the Trinity runs throughout. Feel free to refrain from using the word itself, but if you read and study the Bible, you can, in no way, ignore the concept.

The Holy Spirit helped me to cover my inner turmoil while I was going through. As tired of doing so as I was, I continued to put my happy face on. But, it wasn't until after God spoke to me through His Spirit and told me to invite him to church that the Word of God became my covering. Keep in mind, I still had no faith that this guy would accept my invitation, so my faith was yet not at work. But, after I invited him, I at least knew that some sort of spiritual battle was taking place. The last thing I wanted was to screw up anything that God was doing, so I began leaning on the Word to be my keeper. I do remember praying about the situation and quoting scriptures to keep me reminded that I had put myself out there as an agent who would lead this dude to the sanctuary. I couldn't have him seeing a bad side of mine. It could have scarred him for life. The Word became my weapon of protective covering day in and day out. "Thy word have I hid in mine heart that I might not sin against thee" (Psalm 119:11).

The Word of God protects us in many different ways. It serves as a constant reminder of how we should conduct ourselves in many different types of situations. It always amazes me how one scripture can speak peace and tranquility in the midst of an uproar. Yet another passage can flip your mentality from wrong to right. Perhaps it's because the Word of God is Jesus Christ himself. "And the Word was made flesh, and dwelt among us, (and we beheld his glory, the glory as of the only begotten of the Father,) full of grace and truth" (John 1:14).

When we speak the Word, we are bringing Jesus into the situation at hand. No one is more qualified to help us weather every storm.

It wasn't until the Colorado trip that my faith kicked in to protect me. Although it took nearly a year for my new-found friend to make his way to Jesus, I continued to live the Christian life before him, pray for him, and believe God for his salvation. Hope is a bridge to faith. The conversations we had on the road caused me to hope he would want to be saved. It also gave me a burning desire to want to win that soul for Christ because we developed a relationship and I had begun to genuinely care about him as a person and not just his soul.

What took place is called *personal evangelism*. Some refer to it as *relational evangelism*. Once we built a relationship, he trusted me. His trust in me eventually led to him trusting God. But that relationship worked both ways. Whereas my flesh initially saw him as a waste of time, once we began to build a relationship, my carnal mind shifted. God used our relationship to move my flesh out of the way long enough for my spirit-man to kick in and begin fervently praying for the much-needed deliverance that he wasn't in a condition to pray for by himself.

How often do we allow our flesh to get in the way of our evangelistic efforts? How many times have we been guilty of viewing souls with our flesh rather than through the eyes of God? When will we earnestly expect that God can save any soul? That includes doctors, lawyers, celebrities, professional athletes, politicians, actors, American idols, hip-hop artists, swingers, dope pushers, prisoners, pedophiles, rapists, prostitutes, gang leaders, sorcerers, devil worshipers, serial killers, supremacists, five-percenters, Buddhists, Agnostics, Atheists, and anyone else from your past, present, or future whom you can think of. Even if they are your persecutor, you cannot let the persecution blind you from seeing them through God's eyes.

God gave us those three spiritual coverings to serve as fuel for the battles persecution will bring about. There will be times when the Spirit will direct you to hold your peace. There will be other times that you will need to rise up as a mighty spiritual warrior and fight with all of your strength. Both can be draining. But the encouragement from the Holy Ghost, the inspiration from the Word of God, and the uplifts from your faith will give you all the power you will need to endure. Then, your soul will look back and wonder how you made it over. You'll begin to endure things you thought you'd never be able to endure.

Because of that experience, as well as some others I'll save for future books, I no longer fret in the face of such persecution. I believe God is toughening us for the greater persecution that is ahead. There will come a time when the Christians of the United States of America will be such a minority; the very foundations upon which our country was built will be a faded memory. We will be forced to depend on one another to sustain us as the mark of the beast will be required to buy basic necessities. Everyone will consider us to be fools for not taking the mark and choosing to suffer. But we will have the ultimate victory in the end. That's all that matters. Adopting that mindset will help you mature as a Christian until you have learned to welcome persecution, not with your flesh but through your Spirit.

SEVEN MORE REASONS WHY YOU SHOULD EAT THE SNOW PEAS OF PERSECUTION:

1. People who don't like the taste of peas at all eat snow peas. The pea pods are so dominant; they don't even realize they're eating peas. As you are forced to eat the snow peas of persecution, if you'll munch on the spiritual covering

every step of the way, I promise you, the persecution will pale in comparison.

2. Botanically, snow peas are fruit. That means they are not at all what they look like, smell like or taste like. Thus is the case with persecution. I know it doesn't look or feel like the necessity that it is. But, that doesn't change the fact that it is. At least, now you know.

3. In France, the snow pea is also known as *mangetout* which means "eat it all." The worst thing you can do is partially endure persecution. If you flee that which God has ordained for your life, you'll only be forced to repeat the test again and again until you pass it. In the infamous words of Ms. Sweet Brown, "Ain't nobody got time for that!"

4. Snow peas were native to the Mediterranean region before spreading throughout the world. Religious persecution began against Christians in this same region. It also spread abroad as Christianity spread throughout the world. It baffles me how other religions have been virtually left alone or perhaps only bothered for a period of time. But, Christianity always has been and always will be the seat of global controversy. That's because it is the Truth and Satan can't afford to leave it be. But, we know he's fighting a losing battle. So, I encourage you to be willing to suffer. Your victory has already been won on the cross through Jesus Christ.

5. Although they peak during the warmer times of the year, snow peas are available year-round. When your fervor for God is at its hottest, beware. Your persecution is likely to peak. However, don't be deceived. For even in your most stagnant state, satanic attacks are readily available.

6. Snow peas are higher in Vitamin C than other types of peas. Vitamin C is the vitamin that is well-known for strengthening your immune system. Such is the lasting effect persecution will have on your spiritual life. You'll develop spiritual immunity to the negative connotations associated with enduring such, and you'll celebrate the positive aspects.

7. While Vitamin C may arguably be most famous for promoting immunity, its primary function is the growth, development, and repair of body tissue. Pray for a "no pain, no gain" mentality with regard to persecution.

Here are seven songs I recommend for your meditation and focus regarding persecution:

"I'm Still Here" by Dorinda Clark-Cole

"Through it All" by Andre Crouch

"Bleed the Same" by Mandisa/TobyMac/Kirk Franklin

"Go On Through It" by DeNetria Champ/Vanessa Bell Armstrong

"Still Here" by The Williams Brothers

"I Got Out" by Bryan Popin

"When the Saints" by Sara Groves

CHAPTER SEVEN

Eat Your Proverbs
(The Pigeon Pea)

I t's time for us to eat the pigeon peas of Proverbs. Here, we will learn how to take the advice offered to us in the Word of God. We will examine the author of the book of Proverbs and seek to draw from the principles he used as he governed God's chosen people. We'll also seek to identify common threads within his writings from which we can glean foundational ideologies and apply them to how we live.

Have you ever wondered why pigeon peas are named as such? It's because once upon a time these particular peas were used as feed for pigeons. But, did you know that pigeons and doves are so closely related, they are essentially the same bird? The stereotypical irony is that pigeons are thought of as unintelligible and annoying birds, while doves are highly regarded for their beauty and biblical use as a symbol of the Holy Ghost. Yet, both birds were likely fed the same pigeon peas for food.

The proverbs that we will study in this chapter are uniquely applicable and adaptable to all different types of Christians. While we each have our differences, at the end of the day, we are all Christians and essentially the same. Therefore, we can all benefit from eating the same pigeon peas of proverbs. God depends on us to walk by the same rules and mind the same things. By maintaining high morals and governing our lives by similar principles, we maximize our effectiveness as we promulgate the gospel of Jesus Christ.

A proverb is a short saying that generally states a truth or a word of advice. These adages are respected across the globe. Each inhabited continent can trace its history back to one or more individuals who offered proverbs and were respected for their ability to do so. Many an argument has been had over which part of the ancient world produced the most profound proverbial writers. Feel free to cast your vote for Socrates, Plato, or even Gandhi, if you will. But, govern your life by the proverbs that are found in the Holy Word of God. You may be wondering why I would offer such advice given the fact that the Holy Bible was written by flawed men. However, biblical authors do bear the distinction of having been inspired by God as they wrote. Who's to say that Socrates and Plato were not inspired by God? They very well may have been. But if they were, someone should have told us so. God made sure that everyone knew how the Holy Scriptures came into being:

All scripture is given by inspiration of God, and is profitable for doctrine, for reproof, for correction, for instruction in righteousness. (2 Timothy 3:16)

Knowing this first, that no prophecy of the scripture
is of any private interpretation.
For the prophecy came not in old time by the will of
man: but holy men of God spake as they were moved
by the Holy Ghost. (2 Peter 1:20-21)

While there have been many amazing philosophers throughout time, the Bible exposes some outstanding characteristics to us about King Solomon. He was King David's son and heir to the throne. His qualities first began to show as he went about erecting a temple for God to dwell in. He took it so seriously that he imported the best materials and metals the world had to offer. He would not be satisfied until the highest quality gold, the finest fabrics, and the most precious stones were in place. It was as if nothing was too good for God's temple. Were such an edifice to be constructed today, the silver alone that Solomon imported would cost over twenty billion dollars. Toss in the imported gold and the cost would skyrocket into the hundreds of billions. This mentality impressed God so much so that he offered Solomon anything he wanted. Out of all the things Solomon could have requested, he asked for discernment and an understanding ear to judge God's people. The Israelites were so awesome of a nation that Solomon felt too inadequate to be their king.

You might have observed Solomon erecting this building and called him a fanatic or said that he suffered from obsessive compulsive disorder. You might even say he went overboard or did it all for vain glory. But that's the difference between God and man. Man judges based on what he sees. He judges from the outside in. But God looks solely at the heart. This means, God won't judge you solely based on what you did. He will take into consideration why you did it. And if your motive was pure, correct or justified, He is understanding of your behavior and might even excuse it. Consider this proverb: "Men do not despise a thief, if he steal to satisfy his soul when he is hungry" (Proverbs 6:30).

Let's be frank. Stealing is flat out wrong. We know that "thou shalt not steal" is one of the Ten Commandments (Exodus 20:15). But, Jesus shed some important light on why stealing made the list. When Jesus was questioned about which commandment was the greatest, he explained that all ten hinge on two: Love God with every fiber of your being and love your neighbor as much as you love yourself. The idea is that if I love my neighbor, I won't take anything from him without getting his permission. However, the above proverb causes us to look deeper into the thief's motive. Did he steal the food out of hatred for his brother? Absolutely not. It suggests that were he not hungry, he wouldn't have stolen at all. Was he wrong to steal? Yes, he was. But when you come to understand that his actions were driven by insatiable hunger, you would be less than compassionate to hate him for doing so. He was in a desperate situation. Desperate people tend to do desperate things. Hindsight is 20/20, but the quality of foresight rarely parallels.

Can you see Solomon's 'understanding heart' at work in the above proverb? Only God understands the heart of man to this degree. So, when Solomon asked for an understanding heart, he was requesting a divine impartation. And that was a request that impressed God.

If you are in a leadership position, whether it be in the church, on the job, or in the household as a parent, always endeavor to judge matters with an understanding heart. If your heart seeks to understand, you will refrain from judging until you've gotten all of the facts. Forming such habits will serve you well in your role and gain you much respect as a leader who seeks to serve righteously rather than selfishly and factually rather than subjectively.

I believe that God was able to look into Solomon's heart and see a great deal of passion. Although God made it clear that no building could be great enough to contain Him, He had respect to Solomon's efforts. Solomon had a spirit of excellence when it came to his work for God. Perhaps he inherited this from his father David. Some people are perfectionists by personality. But when it comes to working for God, if your spirit is excellent, you will do your best for Him whether it's deemed perfect or not. It's more about the spirit than the execution. Let us consider this proverb: "Seest thou a man diligent in his business? he shall stand before kings; he shall not stand before mean men" (Proverbs 22:29).

My father used to say, "People find a way to do whatever they want to do." We should want business to be handled well. If we are servants of God, then we should want His business to be handled equally well. This proverb teaches us that if we know what things demand diligence, we will experience favor and elevation. It also suggests that people to whom we may have to answer will have no cause to be angry with us when we remain diligent. Diligence can keep you out of trouble.

Every human being has some set of morals by which they live their lives. The Holy Bible is the foundation that God has authorized from which His people are to build their morals. Encased therein we find the book of Proverbs penned by King Solomon who was inspired by God through his life experiences as a leader, a man, a problem solver, an observer of nature and an observer of animal behaviors. For example, let's read and discuss the first biblical account of Solomon's wisdom in action:

> Then came there two women, that were harlots, unto
> the king, and stood before him.

And the one woman said, O my lord, I and this woman dwell in one house; and I was delivered of a child with her in the house. And it came to pass the third day after that I was delivered, that this woman was delivered also: and we were together; there was no stranger with us in the house, save we two in the house. And this woman's child died in the night; because she overlaid it. And she arose at midnight, and took my son from beside me, while thine handmaid slept, and laid it in her bosom, and laid her dead child in my bosom. And when I rose in the morning to give my child suck, behold, it was dead: but when I had considered it in the morning, behold, it was not my son, which I did bear. And the other woman said, Nay; but the living is my son, and the dead is thy son. And this said, No; but the dead is thy son, and the living is my son. Thus they spake before the king. Then said the king, The one saith, This is my son that liveth, and thy son is the dead: and the other saith, Nay; but thy son is the dead, and my son is the living. And the king said, Bring me a sword. And they brought a sword before the king. And the king said, Divide the living child in two, and give half to the one, and half to the other. Then spake the woman whose the living child was unto the king, for her bowels yearned upon her son, and she said, O my lord, give her the living child, and in no wise slay it. But the other said, Let it be neither mine nor thine, but divide it. Then the king answered and said, Give her the living child, and in no wise slay it: she is the mother thereof. And all Israel heard of the judgment which the king had judged; and they feared the king: for they saw that the wisdom of God was in him, to do judgment. (1 Kings 3:16-28)

People will quickly learn how much wisdom we have when they observe how we respond to controversial situations. It could be that God allowed this initial scandal to surface on the new King's watch that everyone might quickly learn the magnitude of wisdom he possessed. He was faced with two mothers claiming the same child. Simultaneously, he had to solve a murder mystery without having all the facts. One of the two mothers had to be lying. Determining who was telling the truth was the key. A man devoid of wisdom might choose to take a wild guess or flip a coin because in Solomon's day, there was no such thing as DNA testing. So, he was forced to draw from his well of divine wisdom to resolve this matter.

Per the scriptures, the world has its own wisdom and it differs from the wisdom God bestows.

> And my speech and my preaching was not with enticing words of man's wisdom, but in demonstration of the Spirit and of power: That your faith should not stand in the wisdom of men, but in the power of God. Howbeit we speak wisdom among them that are perfect: yet not the wisdom of this world, nor of the princes of this world, that come to nought: But we speak the wisdom of God in a mystery, even the hidden wisdom, which God ordained before the world unto our glory.
> (1 Corinthians 2:4-7)

The wisdom of the world is solely based on knowledge and limited understanding. But, when God imparts wisdom, it reveals things that are not obviously there. Solomon divinely knew that in the face of the death of this child who was yet alive, the real mother would manifest. And it's that level of divine awareness that separates worldly and divine wisdom. Solomon didn't take a gamble hoping the true mother would come forward if he threatened to kill her child. He knew it. Else he wouldn't have taken the chance. This type of wisdom operates in faith and perfect conformity to the revealing power of God.

The late Dr. James W. Jenkins, former Senior Bishop & Chief Overseer of my church organization, was a man of great wisdom. In addition to leading an international church organization, he was both an educator and a shrewd businessman. During his approximate thirty-year tenure, our church organization made great strides in the areas of financial well-being and real estate. However, my most memorable account of him had nothing to do with his business prowess. It had to do with how he exercised evangelical wisdom.

Dr. Jenkins was traveling, as he often did, throughout the nation visiting various churches within the organization. Back then, church officials rarely stayed in hotels. It was an honor and a blessing to invite a constituent of the bishopric into your home even if just for dinner. While he was in Chicago, IL, he found himself in the home of a hard-working church member who was elated to host the chief bishop. However, her husband was unsaved. She desired that her husband come into the church and receive the same gift of the Holy Ghost that she enjoyed. Her attempts to draw him were unfruitful. Dr. Jenkins was up for the task. During and after dinner, Dr. Jenkins showed himself friendly to her husband. The two of them laughed and talked on and on as if they had known each other for years. What this husband failed to realize was that Dr. Jenkins was strategically picking him for information. He was learning all that he could about this man. Somewhere in the course of conversation, Dr. Jenkins struck gold when the husband revealed his love for fishing. Dr. Jenkins made himself the eager student asking multiple questions regarding the sport. It seemed as if once you got this husband to start talking about fishing, he didn't know how to stop. But Dr. Jenkins soaked it all up like a sponge. As they continued to laugh and talk, Dr. Jenkins felt the timing was right to test the temperature of the waters. He invited the husband to be his guest at church the following day as he would be delivering the sermon. They had developed such a solid rapport, it was hard for the husband to justify refusal. So, in the spirit of brotherhood, he agreed to come. Unbeknownst to the husband, Dr. Jenkins had a master plan at work. Perhaps the husband wasn't aware that Jesus and his disciples knew a thing or two about fishing, but he was about to learn. Dr. Jenkins' entire sermon was about fishing. The husband was in awe of how his down-to-earth buddy skillfully infiltrated the techniques of fishing that he'd just taught him a few hours prior into his sermon. The sermon was so interesting that it drew the husband to the Holy Spirit, and his wife was eternally grateful.

Again I'd like to iterate that divine wisdom governed Dr. Jenkins' action plan for winning this soul. It was more than a last-ditch effort. It was a strategic plan that was executed in faith through divine wisdom. Whenever you are faced with a spiritual battle or a controversial situation, never fail to ask God for wisdom in how to handle it. Then, be willing to do exactly what He says and how He says to do it.

While this type of wisdom must come directly from God, I do see a common thread that I feel is worthy of revelation. It seems to me that it's best to deal with the intangibles. That which is intangible has to be more in line with those things that are spiritual, and we serve God with our spirit. God Himself is a spirit. Everything moves by the spirit. If we can affect the spirit-man, the carnal-man will soon follow. Wisdom had Solomon appeal to a mother's love. It influenced her behavior. Wisdom also had Dr. Jenkins appeal to a husband's passion for fishing in a similar manner. If you can deal with a person's heart, you're dealing with the realest part of them; the God part of them. God is love. Love is a spirit. That spirit is real. God is real. People are real. Yet, we make the mistake of appealing to their carnal mind in an effort to effect change in their lives, and either the attempt often fails or is temporary. Next time, let's give wisdom a try.

Solomon felt the need to leave proverbs on record to teach us how to receive, apply and operate through this type of wisdom. The book of Proverbs is also known as the Book of Wisdom. This book of the Bible commences with teaching on wisdom in chapter one and closes with teaching on the same in the book's final chapter. Wisdom is mentioned more than fifty times throughout the book. Below are some of my favorite proverbs regarding wisdom:

> Wisdom is the principal thing; therefore get wisdom: and with all thy getting get understanding. (Proverbs 4:7)

> O ye simple, understand wisdom: and, ye fools, be ye of an understanding heart. (Proverbs 8:5)

> For wisdom is better than rubies; and all the things that may be desired are not to be compared to it. (Proverbs 8:11)

> A man shall be commended according to his wisdom: but he that is of a perverse heart shall be despised. (Proverbs 12:8)

> A scorner seeketh wisdom, and findeth it not: but knowledge is easy unto him that understandeth. (Proverbs 14:6)

Another important facet of the book of Proverbs is how the author teaches us life lessons through the eyes of nature and animals. He took time and observed them, as did Jesus. Everything God placed on planet earth has a purpose and is fulfilling it. When you consider the fact that mankind is doing the total opposite, it's easy to see why we can learn quite a bit from our nonhuman neighbors. One of my favorites details Solomon's observance of the ant.

> Go to the ant, thou sluggard; consider her ways, and be wise: Which having no guide, overseer, or ruler, Provideth her meat in the summer, and gathereth her food in the harvest. How long wilt thou sleep, O sluggard? when wilt thou arise out of thy sleep? (Proverbs 6:6-9)

As you can see, Solomon took his observations of the ant and created proverbial statements to offer advice to those who suffer from slothfulness. I don't know that I've ever seen an ant standing still, unless it was dead. What a perfect example of diligence.

Well, we have a dog. His name is Polo. He is a purebred Maltese that I got for my daughter after she begged for a dog when she was in elementary school. Truth be told, neither my wife nor I wanted a dog. But, I have a hard time saying no to my daughter because she's such a good kid. It's not that I don't love animals. I was rarely without a pet when I was growing up. I'm just keenly aware of the great responsibility that comes with being a pet owner. Furthermore, I was just as keenly aware that my daughter was not ready to undertake such a responsibility. I knew a great deal of caring for this dog would fall on me and my free time is extremely limited. Needless to say, we all love Polo, and he has carved out his own special place in our family. He's a smart dog. I'm always fascinated by his ability to remember everything and forget everything at the same time. He remembers the way back home whenever we walk through the neighborhood regardless of which route we choose. He remembers my family members who come to visit, including those from out of state who rarely come. He remembers the few people whom he dislikes and growls at even if he's only seen them a few times in his entire life. He remembers going to the vet and starts to whimper every time we drive that direction. And of course, he remembers my daughter although she's away at college and can't seem to contain himself whenever she comes home. At the same time, he forgets everything. He forgets how upset I make him when I'm forcing him to take a bath. He forgets the disciplinary actions I put him through when he's disobedient. He has never ever held a grudge for the daily pattern of me leaving him behind while he's begging to go with me. Every time I come back home, he is ecstatic to see me and welcomes me with open arms as if nothing disappointing has ever happened.

If I were to take a stab at writing my own proverb, it would read, "Consider the dog how he readily forgives and replaces dark memories with unconditional love, even for the flawed master." Okay, I'm no Solomon. But, you must admit, a dog's forgiving nature has the makings of a fine proverb that could be used to counsel those who struggle with un-forgiveness or hold grudges. We should take to heart the wisdom Solomon showed by taking note of his surroundings. We, as flawed humans, can learn from those who walk in perfect conformity to God's will.

This rich book covers a wide range of topics including things like jealousy, adultery, love, family, temptation, discipline, faith, money, fools, scorn, integrity, hypocrisy, prosperity, work ethic, poverty, anger, judgement, abominations, and much more. I trust that your appetite is whet enough that you will make it a focal point of your spiritual journey to emulate these principles. The transformation you desire will begin to take shape right before your eyes.

As I close this chapter, I'd like to encourage you to take the proverbial challenge. It was offered to me many years ago during the infancy of my walk with the Lord. Try to read one proverb every day. Try to memorize it and repeat it to yourself throughout the day as frequently as you can. Not only will you be learning

Scripture but you'll be feeding wisdom principles to your spirit. You'll be surprised by the things the Holy Spirit can bring to your remembrance when you need them the most. Help God help you by first helping yourself. Faith without works is dead being alone. But if you regularly feed your spirit with proverbs, you'll have a spiritual database from which to download wisdom when you need it.

SEVEN MORE REASONS WHY YOU SHOULD EAT THE PIGEON PEAS OF PROVERBS:

1. Pigeon peas were fed to the pigeons simply because they were so plentiful. Proverbial wisdom is just as plentiful. God promised to give wisdom liberally to all who ask. So, feel free to eat the pigeon peas of proverbs until your heart is content.

2. Pigeon pea pods change color as they mature. They change from green when young and tender to brown and splotchy when ripening and eventually become a dark purplish color. The inner peas also experience a change in color while maturing. Expect to see recognizable changes in your life as you eat your proverbs. Let this come as no surprise to you as the Word of God is merely doing exactly as it is supposed to.

3. Only when young and tender can pigeon peas be eaten raw, as a snack, added to salads, etc. But if you wait until they have matured, they should be cooked to best enjoy them. Let me encourage you to eat as many of the pigeon peas of proverbs as you can early in your Christian walk, as you first learn of them. Apply them quickly and form good habits now. Don't wait until you're old and settled to try to change. While not impossible, it would have been more easily digestible as a newborn babe.

4. The woody parts of pigeon pea plants make good fire kindling, burning easily when dried. God will use the pigeon peas of proverbs to help transform you into His image when he carries you through His refining Holy Ghost fire. As your fleshly desires burn within the fire, your desire to be more like Him will be solidified with the wisdom He imparts as you change.

5. Peas are cultivated all over the world. However, pigeon peas are most plentifully grown in India where 82% of the world's pigeon peas are cultivated. As you study the Word of God, you'll be blessed in a lot of different ways. But, the book of Proverbs will become your primary source for life application principles and wise sayings to govern your life.

6. While pigeon peas are tough and can grow in just about any atmospheric condition, the one thing that will kill them is frost. Never expect proverbs to flourish within you if your heart is hard and frozen. Be open. Be willing. Get rid of pride and change yourself.

7. We have seen that pigeon peas can be used when young or old and that even the woody part of the plant can be put to use. Also, many animals enjoy the leaves of pigeon pea plants as a food source. Proverbs are beneficial to Christians at all levels of growth and spirituality. They are even beneficial to non-Christians. People from all walks of life respect the wisdom Solomon has left on record and have made their lives better thereby.

Here are seven songs I recommend for your meditation and focus regarding proverbs:

"Word of Life" by Jeremy Camp

"Teach Me Oh Lord" by Vanessa Bell Armstrong

"Speak the Word" by Tina Campbell/Teddy Campbell

"The Law of Confession" by Donald Lawrence

"Sweeter Than The Honeycomb" by Vickie Winans

"Put Your Trust In Jesus" (Proverbs 3:5-6) by Ron Winans Presents Family & Friends Choir II

"Proverbs 4:18-19" by Truth Songs

CHAPTER EIGHT

Eat Your Purpose (The Sugar Snap Pea)

T he final chapter of this book will endeavor to usher you into your life's purpose. You will also discover a convincing argument in favor of God orchestrating each aspect of life to make it possible for each person to realize his individual purpose and walk in it when the time is right. Biblical characters will be scrutinized regarding whether or not they fulfilled their purpose. Finally, this chapter will discuss some specific indicators to help you realize your own purpose and offer some tips on how to begin and succeed as you embark upon this most vital spiritual excursion.

I believe that each soul on this planet has a specific purpose for being here. That purpose is not negated by the fact that most people will never fully realize such. Hence the gratefulness in my heart for serving a patient, long suffering, loving, and forgiving God. For, while we are stumbling aimlessly through life wasting valuable time, God sits on His throne long-sufferingly awaiting a notion that there is more to life than fun and games.

Perhaps at some point you too have asked yourself, "Why did God put me on this planet? How shall my life have meaning? Will I be able to make a lasting impression on the world?" I hope you'll accept my answers to those questions.

Exactly why did God put you on this planet? God put you on this planet to serve Him and Him alone. What differentiates you from the trillions of others who have occupied planet Earth is the unique manner in which He expects you to do so. But, it's not tied up in extreme efforts on your part to outdo your peers or to be greater than any Apostle about whom you've read. Rest assured that before your parents ever knew each other existed, God had already methodically calculated the sum total of every component of your personality. He carefully wove your life's tapestry and tightly connected every fiber of your being. Every cell in your body whether sickled, cancerous, or perfectly normal has a distinct purpose. Every pain you feel is a neurological response to the voice of the Lord God Almighty. Every tear you've had to shed was demanded from the heavens and could not be dried from your eyes until Jehovah Himself ordered the ending. "But even the very hairs of your head are all numbered. Fear not therefore: ye are of more value than many sparrows" (Luke 12:7).

There is no way that God would take the time to assign a separate number to each hair on your head if your life had no purpose. Your life likely means more to Him than it does to you. He views you as an extension of Himself. He made the decision when he stepped out on darkness and created this world that you would occupy it and be fruitful and multiply within it. He was so concerned for your innate tendencies that He knew you wouldn't be content as a puppet in His hands. Therefore, He gave you a choice, trusting that as you feel His love and experience His manifold blessings, you will make the obvious and best choice: to serve Him. He has already given you everything you will need to get started and anything else you'll need along the way has already been promised.

How shall your life have meaning? That depends upon whom it is you allow to make that judgement call. If you ask your parents, they will probably give you a plan descriptive of what their hopes and dreams are for you. If you ask your friends, they may evaluate your life based on how much you have meant to them personally. I would like to invite you to erase personal opinions from your mental list and use the Word of God as the measuring stick. Keep in mind that the Word is Jesus Christ Himself. He wants you to become an asset to the Kingdom of God by living therein and helping it grow. If you can cause one soul to be saved, your life will immediately have unparalleled meaning. But should you selfishly go through life as a Christian who only sought to save himself, not only will your life have no true sense of meaning, but I'm not so certain you'll be welcomed through those pearly gates.

> But ye shall receive power, after that the Holy Ghost
> is come upon you: and ye shall be witnesses unto me
> both in Jerusalem, and in all Judaea, and in Samaria,
> and unto the uttermost part of the earth. (Acts 1:8)

Spreading the Gospel is not optional for Christians. It is their duty and sole purpose in this earth once they have been converted. How can you expect to walk streets of gold when you walked in disobedience to God's command while you were here on the earth? I dare say sinners will be kept out of heaven for their sins of commission while so-called Christians will be kept out of heaven for their sins of omission. Every child of God has a checklist that must be completed before they leave this world and witnessing is atop everyone's list.

Will you be able to make a lasting impression on the world? I'll have to ask you which world you're living in to be able to provide an accurate answer. Once we cross over into Christianity, the things we value are quite opposite from the world's valuation. While they may never view your life-accomplishments as impressive, that soul you brought to Christ will have an impression on the inside equivalent to that of words etched in stone. Your impact in the spirit realm will follow you to the grave and beyond.

> Lay not up for yourselves treasures upon earth, where moth and rust doth corrupt, and where thieves break through and steal: But lay up for yourselves treasures in heaven, where neither moth nor rust doth corrupt, and where thieves do not break through nor steal: For where your treasure is, there will your heart be also. (Matthew 6:19-21)

Before God saved my soul and filled me with the Holy Ghost, I was already working in the church as a child. My parents wouldn't have had it any other way. My gifts became evident pretty early in my life, and I was considered to be a talented kid. I could sing, play musical instruments, orate, act, and discovered a natural ability to dissect harmonies, so I went on to follow in my brother's footsteps and started directing the church choir by age eleven. But, once God filled me with the Holy Ghost, my desire to do His will intensified. I had plans of how we could take the music ministry to another level. Each of my older siblings was a preacher, and I wanted them to start a church so I could erect a music ministry second to none to support them. Imagine my shock when God called me into the ministry. That wasn't part of my plan. Somehow, my intense desire to do God's will didn't feel so intense anymore. Whereas I felt confident in my purpose, I now felt confused and even a tad disappointed.

One mistake a lot of Christians make is thinking that God's purpose for their lives is going to be one particular thing. This very well may not be the case. Spiritually speaking, purpose can be as plural as it is singular. Some people may only have one purpose. But just because God called me into the ministry didn't mean I was wrong about my purpose. Your purpose may expand according to what's needed in the body of Christ during a particular season, and you may have to subsequently execute both. But, learn to listen to the voice of God and walk in obedience to that voice. Personal opinions and beliefs can ring so loudly within that you'll miss the still small voice of God when He speaks. The same God who ordained the major prophets to prophesy for years and years to His people is the same God who snatched up minor prophets and gave many of them one small message to deliver and was done.

It's interesting how God will use your life circumstances to prepare you for your purpose and thrust you into your destiny. The job you currently have could be the training ground for what God needs you to do. That's one of the reasons the book of Proverbs that we previously studied teaches us that out of everything we get, we should get an understanding. (Proverbs 4:7) Try to learn all you can in everything you do. You never know when you may need the Holy Ghost to bring some of those things back to your remembrance.

Joshua was a young man when the Children of Israel first left Egypt on their way to the promised land. Yet, he found himself serving as the minister for Moses, the head man in charge of the exodus. This caused Joshua to observe leadership from an intimate viewpoint. He saw Moses at his spiritual peak. He was right there after Moses encountered God's glory, which caused his face to glow so brightly it had to be veiled before the people could draw nigh unto him. He also saw Moses at his worst, when he was overcome with anger and broke the tablets upon which God had written the Ten Commandments with His own finger. He witnessed Moses punishing the people when he pulverized their idolatrous golden calf, sprinkled the gold dust into their water, and made them drink of it. He witnessed Moses work the miracle of producing enough water from a rock to quench the thirst of all the tens of thousands of people in the twelve tribes of Israel.

Joshua experienced the pangs of empathetic pastoring as he stood by God's anointed. Clearly, these experiences prepared him for his purpose which was to take over the leadership position after the death of his mentor, Moses. Joshua did a stellar job as the leader—and rightfully so. Considering all that he experienced and witnessed, he had no excuse for failure. Furthermore, he knew firsthand that God's favor would be with him. I love the way Joshua boldly stood in faith when others were doubtful that the children of Israel would be able to overtake those who were occupying the promised land when they arrived. He didn't see God's people as tiny grasshoppers in the eyes of giant enemies. All he focused on were the victories God had already wrought for them. It fueled his feistiness. He wanted to fight and expected God to bring triumph. Nothing else mattered. With this type of faith, I would say Joshua passed his first test with flying colors.

Remember to glean all you can from your current situation. Observe everything. Take note of the positives as well as the negatives. Understand that everything God allows in your life has its own purpose, and it could be preparing you for yours. You can learn from the mistakes of others. You can also put together a beautiful puzzle of pieces you pick up along life's way. Experience is a good teacher. I never realized how much my former pastor had poured into me while I was serving as her assistant until I became a pastor myself. Even other people noticed some similarities. I'm still uniquely me. But, I wouldn't be all that I am, were it not for those under whom I sat.

Bishop Thomas used to tell us as young staff ministers that she expected us to be greater than she was. To me, that sounded impossible. But she explained that we should be greater because we have everything God gave us in addition to the things God gave her that she was pouring into us. She was telling us if we take in what we are being taught, in time, we can't help but become greater. Being greater was never my goal. My honor would be to pale in comparison. Yet, while I was faithfully sitting in my usual seat (center of the front pew) for Wednesday Night Bible Study soaking up knowledge like a sponge in hopes of fulfilling my purpose, I was concerned about some of my colleagues across our national church organization who had chosen other paths. Some became backsliders for various reasons. Some were running full speed ahead on a fast track to realize their dreams. Others seemingly had all the answers and no one could tell them anything. There were those who felt God had anointed them to lead while in the days of their youth and felt as though they should have been leading long before. It was painful to watch those who couldn't seem to prosper in their ministry work no matter how hard they tried. Others flourished for a season only to see their works crumble for one reason or another.

While God didn't give me a spirit of fear, it was a fear of failure that eventually kept me grounded. I say "eventually" because I too had my share of failures. Embarrassing failures, indeed. I endured everything from extreme marital strife to being arguably the smartest in my family never to finish college. Not to mention the demons of my sinful past that Satan assigned to destroy my marriage, my character, my spiritual walk with God, and even my mental stability. But, I managed to defeat Satan and am now finally beginning to rise above it all. I see things through different lenses now. All of these things are coming together as tiny pieces of my purpose. I'm certain that part of my purpose is to serve God's people as a pastor. Pastors have to touch every facet of people's lives. From the christening to the eulogy, the pastor is there. My wife and I wouldn't be able to counsel couples who are on the brink of divorce had we not already faced that ugly monster. I'm still shocked at how much they sound like us less than five minutes into a session. Some of the things people have confessed to me I'll have with me to my grave. But, because I've been at my own lowest low, nothing shocks me anymore, and I never look down on them or think any less of them. I know how to build them back up. But had I not been there, I might have handled things differently.

I've learned to praise God that He allowed me to go through some heavy things early in life and helped me to learn from each adversity. Some of the lessons were slow and hard, but I still learned them. I'm just glad I did so before it was too late. Throughout the learning process, the devil often tried to tell me that it was too late for me to ever turn the corner. But, he was just doing what he always does. He lies. He's a liar. It's who he is. He fathered lying in the Garden of Eden and has been proficiently producing lies ever since. Expect nothing less from him.

Judas learned a hard lesson, but by the time he learned, it was too late. The Bible depicts him as embarrassed and remorseful after betraying Jesus. But how do you reverse a murder? The mental torment was too much for him to emotionally bear, so he took his own life as a swap out for having been responsible for helping the authorities take Jesus' life. I believe that because God knows our future and what our end will be, He can use various lives as examples to others. What if God in His omniscience knew that had

Judas lived, he would have fallen back into sin anyways? What if betrayal was in his soul, and had it not been Jesus, it would have eventually been one of the other eleven disciples? As followers, we have to believe that God is always just. But whether we like it not, the Bible disclosed to us the fate of Judas for a reason. It behooves us to flee the unyielding chains of reprobation lest we bear the same fate as he.

> And even as they did not like to retain God in their knowledge, God gave them over to a reprobate mind, to do those things which are not convenient; Being filled with all unrighteousness, fornication, wickedness, covetousness, maliciousness; full of envy, murder, debate, deceit, malignity; whisperers, Backbiters, haters of God, despiteful, proud, boasters, inventors of evil things, disobedient to parents, Without understanding, covenant breakers, without natural affection, implacable, unmerciful: Who knowing the judgment of God, that they which commit such things are worthy of death, not only do the same, but have pleasure in them that do them. (Romans 1:28-32)

If God turns you over to a reprobate mind, you're sure to miss your purpose. Your heart will no longer want to seek it. Sin will utterly consume you, and all hope for redemption will be lost. If you are still tampering with sinful nature, meditate on the above scripture and realize that God, while longsuffering, must end the game you're playing at some point. If you are not inclined to pursue your purpose, He will have to assign it to someone else; and that assignment starts in the womb.

> Before I formed thee in the belly I knew thee; and before thou camest forth out of the womb I sanctified thee, and I ordained thee a prophet unto the nations. (Jeremiah 1:5)

How many years or decades has God wasted waiting on you to get serious about your purpose? Your silence could sound like screams in the ears of God. By failing to choose, you may have passively cast a vote that cannot be reversed once the angels have tallied and recorded it on high. Let me urge you to be *transformed by the renewing of your mind* as soon as possible. Don't force God to reassign the work He's entrusted to you.

I'd like to offer two suggestions that will help you realize what your purpose is. The first and foremost thing you must do is ask God, not necessarily expecting an immediate verbal response. But making sure you don't fall into the category of individuals who are wondering but never took the time to sincerely consult the all-knowing God. When you ask God, don't just ask open-ended questions such as, "What is my purpose? What do you want me to do with my life?" Ask God to make His divine will for your life clear. Ask Him to manifest Himself in the areas of your life that He has anointed so that they will stand out among everything else that you do. Request that the Holy Spirit respond as a witness. Ask Him to make it known to others as well. Invite Him to instruct you and guide you down the right paths toward your divine purpose.

Finally, make sure you don't already know and are in denial. Never forget that this choice is up to you. Instead of expecting God to beg you, take a retrospective glance over your life. Were there times when you felt God was urging you to do something or move in a particular direction? How did that feel? Ask God to renew those moments and to give you a heart to obey and be in tune with His Spirit. And don't be afraid to try a few things. God loves willing workers. Many people have found their niche through trial and error. If you're good at it, and you can do it to help build God's Kingdom, why not do it?

> Whatsoever thy hand findeth to do, do it with thy
> might; for there is no work, nor device, nor knowl-
> edge, nor wisdom, in the grave, whither thou goest.
> (Ecclesiastes 9:10)

It's entirely possible that you could be facing a Jonah-like situation. Just because you don't want to do it doesn't mean God
doesn't need you to do it. It's equally possible that you could be
facing a Saul-like situation. You may have been deceived by the
enemy into thinking that you're walking in your purpose when
it could be that God wants you to do the direct opposite. If this
is the case, do not worry. As long as your heart is as sincere as
Saul's was when he was on Damascus Road, the same God will
stop you in your tracks and place your feet on Straight Street
in due season. Unfortunately, many Christians will have to face
Joseph-like situations. Your purpose could be so grandiose that
it likely will not come full circle without some blood, sweat, and
tears. But, if you can trust God through the entire process, He
will make the enemy your footstool even if the enemy is within
your own family. Joseph went through seven p's of his own to get
to the place of his purpose:

1. He started in the **PIT** from where his brothers sold him.

2. He was purchased by **POTIPHER**.

3. He wound up in the house where **PHARAOH'S WIFE** lied
   on him and got him in all kinds of trouble with his boss.

4. He got thrown into **PRISON**.

5. After interpreting Pharaoh's dreams, he was finally given
   a job in the **PALACE**.

6. To keep his heart pure, he was positioned by God to have
   to not only forgive his brothers for selling him into slavery

but had to bless his enemies by making great **PROVISIONS** for them so they not perish during the famine.

7. And finally, after a short reconciliation, he had to grieve the **PASSING** of his father; the one who gave him the coat of many colors that led to this colorful life he now led.

At the end of the day, the passion behind pursuing your purpose must come from within. I pray that you will discover an insatiable appetite for the peas of purpose and make Jesus proud to own you before His Father which is in heaven.

SEVEN MORE REASONS WHY YOU SHOULD EAT THE SUGAR SNAP PEAS OF PURPOSE:

1. Sugar snap peas are a cross between green peas and snow peas. So before your life can yield the sugar snap peas of purpose, expect the snow peas of persecution to bring you to the green peas of prayer. Once these two intersect, you just might stumble into your purpose.

2. In 1979, sugar snap peas won the AAS Edible Vegetable All American National Gold Medal. Purpose is reserved for relentless fighters who will accept nothing less than victory. When you finally walk into your purpose, you will have won the coveted prize.

3. Sugar snap peas are only available February through May which is one third of the year. So, don't be surprised if you spend twice as much time searching for your purpose than you do indulging it.

4. During winter months, sugar snap peas are generally bigger and sweeter, while in the warmer months, they are small and lack flavor. Make sure your purpose shines its brightest during the darkest areas of your life. This is when Jesus is putting you on center stage for the entire

world to see. Don't make Him ashamed. Do Him proud. Be confident in who God called you to be.

5. Whether young and tender or overripe, sugar snap peas never have to be separated from their pod to be enjoyed. Everything in your life that came together to push you into your purpose will always be there for you to pull from. You can even embrace the pain. It helped to make you the strong victor you are today.

6. Unlike many other vegetables, sugar snap peas tend to maintain their color throughout the cooking process. After you discover your purpose, you'll still go through periods of life when Satan will turn up the heat and try to run you out of the kitchen. Stand your ground in the faith and confidence of what God commanded you to do and hold fast. Don't change. Don't second guess. Don't be a spiritual chameleon. Be what you are and live the life.

7. Although encased in a pod, this hybrid is string-less and therefore has no part needing to be discarded prior to consumption. Even if your purpose winds up being a multi-faceted spiritual hybrid of things, don't discard any aspect of it. Do it all to the glory and honor of God. If He gave you a plethora of abilities, He expects you to use all of them (Luke 12:47-48).

Here are seven songs I recommend for your meditation and focus regarding purpose:

1. "God's Up to Something" by Jason Crabb

2. "It's Your Time" by Luther Barnes

3. "My Destiny" by Fred Hammond

4. "I Know the Plans" by Martha Munizzi

5. "Go Get It" by Mary Mary

6. "My Purpose" by The Williams Brothers

7. "Destiny" by VaShawn Mitchell

Carter's Black-Eyed Peas & Rice

1 pound of dried black-eyed peas
1 tablespoon Creole seasoning (such as Tony Chachere's®)
2 tablespoons of kosher salt
1 tablespoon vegetable oil or shortening
1 pound smoked beef sausage (such as Hillshire Farms) cut into
1/2-inch chunks
1 large onion, finely chopped
1 green bell pepper, finely chopped
4 ribs celery, finely chopped
4 medium cloves of garlic, minced or chopped
½ to 1 tablespoon of cayenne pepper (to taste; optional)
1 teaspoon ground sage
½ teaspoon of sugar
2 teaspoons of ground black pepper
1 smoked turkey wing portion (I use the large portion of the
flapper)
4 sprigs fresh thyme
3 bay leaves
¼ stick of butter
Cooked white or brown rice, for serving

Place beans in a large bowl or pot and cover with 6 cups of cold water. Add 2 tablespoons kosher salt and stir until dissolved. Set aside at room temperature overnight. Drain and rinse the next morning.

In a large heavy pot, heat the vegetable oil or shortening over medium-high heat. Add the sausage and stir fry until it starts to form a browned crust. Add onions, bell peppers, and celery. Add the creole seasoning, cayenne pepper and black pepper and cook until vegetables have softened. Add the garlic and sage and cook until fragrant; about 1 additional minute. Add beans and smoked turkey wing portion along with enough water to cover them by about 2 inches. Also add the sugar, thyme, and bay leaves. Bring to a boil and reduce to a simmer. Add the butter and stir until melted. Cover and cook until beans are completely tender. Check them every ½ hour and stir well. Check more frequently if your pot causes them to stick to the bottom. Do not let this happen. Stir as often as necessary from the bottom. May take 2 to 3 hours. Once the turkey is tender, feel free to remove the bone if desired. You can also remove the tender wing, debone it, shred or chop the meat and return the meat to the pot.

Remove lid and continue to cook, stirring occasionally, until liquid has lessened and the dish has thickened and turned creamy. Add water a ½ cup at a time if necessary. Repeat as necessary until desired level of creaminess is achieved. Discard bay leaves and thyme stems. Add more creole seasoning to your desired taste. For best texture, let cool and refrigerate overnight. Reheat the next day, adding a little water to loosen to desired consistency. Serve over steamed white rice. This dish pairs well with cornbread.

BIBLIOGRAPHY

http://www.foodreference.com/html/fblackeyedpea.html

http://en.wikipedia.org/wiki/Chickpea

http://www.softschools.com/facts/plants/chickpea_facts/1087/

http://www.funtrivia.com/en/subtopics/The-Humble-Chickpea-308671.html

https://www.thedailymeal.com/broccoli-actually-most-kids-favorite-vegetable

https://www.quora.com/How-many-peas-are-there-in-an-average-pea-pod

https://www.littlegreene.com/pea-green

https://www.almanac.com/plant/peas

https://www.thefactsite.com/2013/08/interesting-pea-facts.html

http://thelocalpalate.com/articles/a-field-guide-to-field-peas/

http://www.mbsinc.com/tithing-considerations-for-business-owners/

https://www.daveramsey.com/askdave/stewardship/tithing-on-a-business

https://web.sonoma.edu/users/d/daniels/chinaproverbs.html

https://en.wikipedia.org/wiki/Proverb

http://www.specialtyproduce.com/produce/Snow_Peas_425.php

http://www.thefreedictionary.com/pigeon+pea

http://www.specialtyproduce.com/produce/Sugar_Snap_Peas_5055.php

https://all-americaselections.org/product/pea-sugar-snap/

http://www.whfoods.com/genpage.php?pfriendly=1&tname=foodspice&dbid=55

http://www.encyclopedia.com/doc/1G2-3429800014.html Black Eyed Peas

Contemporary Musicians | 2004 | Sanchez, Brenna | 700+ words | Copyright

http://lubbockonline.com/gardening/2013-12-31/peffley-black eyed-peas-good-luck-food-comes-civil-war#. U4ElMvldWSp Peffley: Black-eyed peas as good luck food comes from Civil War

Posted: December 31, 2013 - 8:27pm | Updated: January 1, 2014 - 1:06am by Ellen Peffley

The Holy Bible – King James Version

ABOUT THE AUTHOR

W illiam Carter, Jr. has been teaching and preaching the Gospel for over twenty years. His pastorate experience spans over a decade, and he remains in high demand traveling extensively as a keynote speaker, workshop facilitator, and revivalist. Known for cleverly telling the pointed truth, his ministry has carried him behind prison walls, into homeless shelters, across radio airwaves, on social media outlets, and even to street corners with a bullhorn to shamelessly preach the unadulterated Word of God. Considered a child prodigy, having composed his first song at age three, Carter later left his footprint in the Christian music industry as a Dove Award nominated songwriter and has performed for some of Christian music's top artists including Margaret Becker and Larnelle Harris. To name a few in the Gospel music industry, Carter has shared the stage with Gospel music legends like

Shirley Caesar, sang background for industry staples such as Hezekiah Walker, opened for chart toppers like Kierra Sheard and sat under the tutelage of trend setters such as Kirk Franklin. His multidimensional writing ability allowed him to pen and produce stage plays, write for online magazines, work as a Gospel music CD reviewer and publish his interviews with professional Gospel/Christian artists. He is the senior pastor at the House of God Church in Nashville, Tennessee where he resides with his lovely wife Nova, talented daughter Aijalon, and loyal dog Polo. In his spare time he enjoys watching sports, traveling, cooking, and playing games with family and close friends. https://www.facebook.com/WilliamBCarterJr/

www.ingramcontent.com/pod-product-compliance
Lightning Source LLC
Chambersburg PA
CBHW060433090426
42733CB00011B/2254